P9-CKE-636

# Wives of the Presidents

by
Arden Davis Melick

HAMMOND
INCORPORATED

# Acknowledgments

Many people and organizations have given invaluable assistance in the preparation of this book. The author and the publisher are deeply grateful to the following for their help in research and arranging special access to the White House and special collections of presidential memorabilia:

Office of the White House: Special Assistants to the President—John Davies and Dwight Chapin
The White House: Curator Clement E. Conger
White House Historical Association: Executive Director Hillory A. Tolson
Smithsonian Institution: Barbara J. Coffee
National Gallery of Art: Allison Luchs, Katherine Warwick, Jane Wallace
National Portrait Gallery: Mona Dearborn
National Trust for Historic Preservation: Mrs. Charles Stewart
The Brooklyn Museum: Linda Ferber
Chicago Historical Society: Mary Frances Rhymer
Museum of the City of New York: Charlotte La Rue
New-York Historical Society: Wilson G. Duprey
Dwight D. Eisenhower Library: John E. Wickman
James Monroe Memorial Foundation: Ingrid W. Hoes
James Knox Polk Memorial Auxiliary: Harriette J. Quin
Woodrow Wilson House: Ruth L. Dillon
Maplewood Memorial Library: Helen V. D. Winter and staff
Centenary College for Women: President Edward W. Seay, Ruth Scarborough
Mary McRae Hood
Virginia Heller Keiley
Phyllis Jenkins Polhemus

WIVES OF THE PRESIDENTS, Revised Edition
Entire contents © copyright 1972, 1977 by HAMMOND INCORPORATED
All rights reserved. No part of this book may be reproduced or utilized in any form or by any means, electronic or mechanical including photocopying, recording or by any information storage and retrieval system, without permission in writing from the publisher.

Library of Congress Cataloging in Publication Data
Melick, Arden Davis.
    Wives of the Presidents.
    Bibliography: p.
    Includes index.
    1. Presidents — United States — Wives — Biography. I. Title.
E176.2.M44    1977    973'.0992    [B]    75-142940

ISBN 0-8437-3813-8
ISBN 0-8437-3913-4 lib. bdg.

Printed in United States of America

# Contents

# 1
## Martha Washington

### The General's Lady

DETAIL FROM PAINTING BY DANIEL HUNTINGTON,
THE BROOKLYN MUSEUM

There was no rejoicing at Mount Vernon when the messenger brought the news. It was April 1789, and George Washington had been elected first President of the United States. Martha's round hazel eyes clouded with the prospect of once more sharing her husband with his country. The end of the struggle for independence had brought peace to America, but not to George and Martha Washington. They neither sought public acclaim nor welcomed it, but with resolve bordering on stoicism accepted their responsibilities. The honor attending the presidency meant little to Martha. With it, her "lost years" began.

Martha Washington took no part in the triumphant welcome and extravagant reception the city of New York gave her husband on Inauguration Day. Hoping to give his "dearest Patsy" a gentle introduction to public life, George wanted to be "well fixed" at the seat of government on the Hudson before sending for her. Waiting quietly at Mount Vernon, Martha gave grave consideration to her new role as the wife of the President of the United States. The new nation was held together by slender threads that could easily snap under stress, and Martha knew it would be difficult to please both anti-royalists and those who preferred very formal behavior from the chief of state.

Lady Washington was well-received indeed. Although she might have regretted privately that it was a plump, aging grandmother the public saw rather than the neat-figured girl she had once been, Martha was admired nevertheless. Nearing sixty, her lovely complexion and white, even teeth were still worthy of comment. Her snowy hair, fragrant with powder, was piled becomingly high, or tucked beneath a ribboned cap. Abigail Adams, wife of the vice-president, was deeply impressed with Mrs. Washington, commenting on Martha's "elegant plainness" of dress and "modest dignified manners."

BUREAU OF ENGRAVING AND PRINTING

Mount Vernon,
stately mansion where George Washington
brought his bride in 1759.

The "plan of living" that George had hoped everyone would find reasonable involved a weekly levee Tuesday afternoons, a Thursday dinner party, and Friday receptions at which Martha presided, with even George just a guest. She found that, as a social capital, New York suffered by comparison with Williamsburg and Philadelphia. Then, too, she felt restricted by the decisions she and George had made regarding the example they must set. Confessing that she felt "more like a state prisoner than anything else," Martha declared: "There is certain bounds set for me, which I must not depart from — and as I cannot do as I like, I am obstinate and stay at home a great deal."

Martha regarded the friendship of Abigail Adams as an unexpected bonus in otherwise dull New York. Martha had considered Abigail's intellect superior to her own, and was perhaps concerned that her company would not be sufficiently stimulating for Mrs. Adams. To their mutual delight, the two found they had a great deal in common and enjoyed one another's company enormously.

Martha was well aware that most people regarded her husband with awe, if not reverence. She knew, too, that his real character, talents, and shortcomings were already shrouded in legend, and that no one would ever know him as she did. What she may not have realized was the fact that her own place in history would be both romanticized and disparaged.

There were many who speculated that the marriage between George Washington and the wealthy twenty-seven-year-old widow of Daniel Parke Custis was merely a union of convenience. During the following forty years, however, sceptics had ample time to reconsider. Before George's marriage it had been rumored that his heart belonged to Sally Fairfax, the wife of George William Fairfax, Washington's dear friend. Whatever the gos-

sip, it meant little to Martha. Sally was indeed witty and delightful, but utterly devoted to her husband. Their estate, Belvoir, had been almost a second home to George in his youth, where he had often said he spent the happiest days of his life. As far as a romance with Sally was concerned, Martha saw no reason for jealousy. It was undeniable that George had become completely committed to Martha just a few months after their chance meeting at the home of a mutual friend. Soon after their engagement, as he left for a last campaign fighting the French, he wrote to Martha:

I embrace the opportunity to send a few words to one whose life is now inseparable from mine. Since that happy hour when we made our pledges to each other, my thoughts have been continually going to you as to another self.

Martha did indeed become his other self. A creamy confection in white satin and pearls, Martha Dandridge Custis wed George Washington January 6, 1759. She was just chest-high to her strapping husband, who took pleasure in her daintiness, referring to her feet as "the smallest fives." She was the mistress he felt Mount Vernon deserved, enriching it not only with her own lands, but bringing to it her considerable domestic abilities. She herself taught the slaves to spin and also instructed them in the cooking of her excellent recipes. In a time when needlework, plain and fancy, was a necessary and popular feminine skill, Martha was almost without peer. Medicines from her herb garden and pungent onion-and-molasses cough syrup were well-regarded remedies. George's careful management of his estate was beautifully complemented by Martha's contribution to its continued thriving.

Young Martha Dandridge had, after all, been trained for the role of a Virginia squire's

NEW-YORK HISTORICAL SOCIETY

While in New York
the Washingtons lived in this house
on Cherry Street.

wife. Her education was limited to that which was considered sufficient for a fashionable young lady of Tidewater Virginia. She was well-versed in the social graces of dancing, polite conversation, and music as well as the practical skills of running a home. At seventeen she became the bride of Colonel Daniel Parke Custis. Her bridegroom, then in his mid-thirties, took her home to his plantation on the Pamunkey River. They had a happy, growing family, but two of their children died in infancy. Suddenly Daniel, too, passed away. At twenty-five, more girl than matron, Martha was a widow with a small son and daughter.

There were suitors, naturally, when the period of mourning for Daniel was over, but the gentle giant from Mount Vernon outshone them all. He had captivated not only Martha but her children as well. They were to be his only family, and when Patsy died in her teens and Jacky as a young man, George's grief nearly matched Martha's. Their disappointment in having no children of their own was cloaked in concern for those of their relatives, culminating with George's adoption of Jacky's children. Over the years, Martha and George made a home for a stream of nephews, nieces, and grandchildren, feeling young themselves when surrounded by children.

As time passed, Martha's dream of a tranquil life at Mount Vernon with her husband seemed more out of reach than ever. Personal tragedies, however, paled beside the plight of the colonies. Events across the land and even in the House of Burgesses in Williamsburg made it clear that war with England was more than a remote possibility. The situation grew still worse with a stamp tax, a tax on tea, and shocking news of violence in Boston. Martha knew that the Apollo Room of the Raleigh Tavern had become more of a council chamber than social gathering place, and George would clearly

be in the center of things when final action was taken. Martha was resigned to his decision to serve in the Continental Congress in Philadelphia, but it was more difficult to accept the fact that he would head the Continental Army. Breaking the news of his appointment to his wife, George wrote:

I should enjoy more happiness in one month with you at home than I have the most distant prospect of finding abroad, if my stay were to be seven times seven years.

The eight years that followed were years of separation each spring, when George's army broke camp to meet or engage the enemy, and winter reunions wherever his headquarters was established. Martha, who had been one of the first Virginia women to give up tea and fancy English yard goods for unsatisfactory coffee and homespun dresses, clearly continued to support the patriot cause in whatever way she could. Her intentions were simple but courageous. She would follow George wherever and whenever she could in an effort to comfort and encourage him and his men.

Elated when George sent for her from Cambridge, Massachusetts, Martha eagerly set out with a carriage filled with hampers of Mount Vernon food, and yarn, needles, thread and cloth tucked into every available space. As commander in chief, George took the responsibility of planning her journey to the last detail, leaving to Martha the decisions of what to bring.

Life at headquarters gave Martha the opportunity to do something, at last, to show her support of the patriot cause. She organized the officers' wives and neighborhood ladies into sewing groups that took charge of the soldiers' clothing. She helped nurse the wounded in the camp hospitals and provided food from her own pantries for the men. When staff shortages were acute, Martha

THE GRANGER COLLECTION

This was the Presidential Mansion while Philadelphia was the nation's capital from 1790 to 1800.

offered her services as a secretary. With smiling apologies for her penmanship, she prepared copies of orders and other official documents. Totally discreet, she had her husband's complete trust. Professing total ignorance of the cabals and intrigues surrounding George, she stopped idle gossip by claiming to know nothing whatever.

Each bitter winter of the war found Martha at George's side. She hurried to Morristown, New Jersey, where she found her husband lying seriously ill. At Arnold's Tavern, west of the green, she personally cared for his every need, competently nursing him back to health.

A superior horsewoman, Martha loved to accompany George when he rode through the Jersey hills, catching glimpses from time to time of the British across the river in New York. Her presence did a great deal to cheer the solemn commander. General Greene observed "Mrs. Washington is extremely fond of the General and he of her; they are happy with each other."

There was less reason for cheer at Valley Forge, where Martha wept for the freezing soldiers and tried to comfort George in his anguish for them. A blazing Mount Vernon hearth was surely a more appropriate place for a middle-aged grandmother to spend the winter than Valley Forge, numbing Jockey Hollow, or Newburgh.

She shared victory, too, only to have Yorktown's triumph turn to tragedy before her eyes with the death of her son. Less accustomed even than his mother to army life, Jacky had insisted on seeing Cornwallis surrender, then succumbed himself of camp fever.

The end of the war only meant the beginning of more absences from Mount Vernon, these in the interests of putting the new nation on as firm a footing as possible. Never blind to the esteem in which other men held her

husband, Martha listened and waited as always, wondering what more they would ask of him, and knowing, too, that whatever they asked, he would do if he could.

Martha, too, did whatever was asked of her. She set an impeccable precedent as First Lady, dignifying the new democracy. When the capital moved to Philadelphia, she was more at ease in her role. The Market Street mansion Robert Morris had put at their disposal was more comfortable than their New York quarters. Philadelphia society was considerably more lively, too, and Martha bowed to its customs by extending her Friday receptions until 10:00 P.M. instead of the earlier hour of 9:00. She even indulged in a little matchmaking, urging Dolley Todd, a charming Quaker widow, to accept the marriage proposal of long-time bachelor James Madison.

Martha was delighted when Washington's Farewell Address, written and rewritten so many times, was finally made public. She was not sorry that another president would be the first to live in the new federal city rising on the banks of the Potomac. His countrymen wept when her husband stepped down, leaving John Adams to fill a seemingly abyss-like void. Martha sympathized, but felt no regrets.

Mount Vernon waited for them, beckoned to them and claimed them at last. They had just two more years together, "Farmer" Washington, as George thought of himself, and Martha, confessing her joy to be once more "an old fashioned Virginia housekeeper." With George's death in December 1799, part of Martha died too. She closed the blue and white bed chamber they had shared for forty years and took a small garret room for herself. Before her death in 1802, she carefully burned nearly all of George's letters to her. She had shared enough of him with his country and would share no more.

11

# 2
## Abigail Adams

### First Lady of Liberty

At home in Quincy, Massachusetts, Abigail Adams had awaited the results of the bitter campaign of 1796. John's election was the crowning achievement of a life dedicated to his country, yet she did not glory in the honor that was now theirs. She left no doubt about her sentiments, writing to John:

My feelings are not those of pride or ostentation upon the occasion. They are solemnized by a sense of the obligations, the important trusts and numerous duties connected with it. That you may be enabled to discharge them with honor to yourself, with justice and impartiality to your country, and with satisfaction to this great people, shall be the daily prayer of your A.A.

The highly respected, fashionable matron who became First Lady in 1797 bore little resemblance to the slender, chestnut-haired minister's daughter John Adams had married thirty-three years before. Parson and Mrs. William Smith of Weymouth, Massachusetts, would never have foreseen such a future for their Abigail. In fact, they had been reconciled, though far from enthusiastic, when she chose to marry John Adams. Admittedly, John was brilliant, industrious and devoted to their daughter. But he was a lawyer, and the law as a profession was not considered entirely respectable. Parson Smith would have much preferred a clergyman for a son-in-law.

However, Abigail and John were deeply in love, their mutual affection ripening during a three-year courtship. John, never adept at flattery or small talk, was fully at ease with the intellectual Miss Smith. Her love of books and study was equal to his own, although, delicate as a child, she had not been allowed to attend school. Tutored at home by her father, she had developed an insatiable appetite for learning. Current political events, too, intrigued her, an interest that had been sparked by her Grandfather

Quincy. As the speaker of the Massachusetts House of Representatives, he entertained the Bay Colony's leading men at his home. There Abigail had listened to long discussions of domestic and foreign affairs. Her knowledge of the basic differences between England and the colonies grew with John's, and they spent many hours talking about ways to resolve them. Together, they would implement many of their ideas in the establishment of a new nation.

John Adams brought his bride to a saltbox cottage in Braintree (later known as Quincy). Abigail stretched John's meager legal fees as far as possible, managing to live mostly on what they could produce on their own modest property. Realizing that his wife was a formidable household economizer, John soon trusted her completely to budget their finances. Later, during John's long absences in the service of his country, Abigail's frugality and sharp business sense kept them on a sound financial footing.

Just a year after her marriage, Abigail met the first test of loyalty to the political ideals she and John professed. John had helped lead a boycott against the Stamp Act, succeeding so well in uniting opposition to the detested legislation that England retaliated by closing all the courts. With all legal offices shut down, John could not practice law. Despite the blow to their income, Abigail did not complain. Instead, she encouraged John to continue in the course they had originally charted for themselves.

In 1768 Abigail moved to Boston with three-year-old Abigail, nicknamed Nabby, and year-old John Quincy. The courts were open again, and John's business was thriving. So was the patriot cause. Boston was fast becoming a hotbed of rebellion. From her house in Brattle Square Abigail watched the first hated Redcoats march into town and later heard the shots of the "Boston Massacre." As

Abigail Adams was never far from the center of action as British-American differences flamed into open rebellion.

John's commitment to opposing England grew, so did Abigail's knowledge of the form that opposition would take. She was well aware that plans were afoot to cope with quantities of tea the British had shipped to the port of Boston. She wrote to a friend, "Tea, that baneful weed, is arrived. Great and I hope effectual opposition has been made to the landing of it. . .I tremble when I think what may be the consequences."

The consequences were more far-reaching than she might have guessed. In response to the dumping of the tea, England shut down the busy seaport of Boston and transferred the Bay Colony's government to Salem. However, Tory sympathizers found to their dismay that the king's actions had only stirred up more resentment, further unifying the colonies. They came to the aid of stricken Massachusetts with food and money for relief, as well as official statements of support. In Williamsburg, Virginia, the House of

PAINTING BY GILBERT STUART, NATIONAL GALLERY OF ART, WASHINGTON, D.C.

Burgesses had been dissolved by an angry governor, but concerned delegates met later at the Raleigh Tavern, proposing an annual congress of all the colonies. By September 1774 the First Continental Congress was ready to convene in Philadelphia.

Abigail moved back to Braintree, proud that John was to be a delegate to the congress, although she did not relish being separated from him. It was clear she put the needs of the colonies above her own, writing to John, "Uncertainty and expectation leave the mind great scope. Did ever any kingdom or state regain its liberty when once it was invaded, without bloodshed?...I long to have you on the site of action."

She was correct in predicting bloodshed. One budding April day, a rider shouted news of fighting on the Lexington Green. Events at Lexington and Concord incensed the colonies. John deplored the violence, but prepared for the Second Continental Congress with the hope that delegates at last would be convinced that they had no alternative but to declare independence. Abigail remained at home, doing all she could to help those already fighting and dying in Massachusetts. She fed militiamen who straggled across her fields and nursed the wounded, dragging mattresses into the kitchen or John's law office when the barn was filled to overflowing with weary soldiers. She took in refugees from Boston, whose property had been confiscated by the British, knowing that at any moment she herself might have to flee with Nabby, John Quincy, little Charles and baby Thomas.

She wrote often to John in Philadelphia, telling all she could of news at home and on the battlefield. No stranger to gunfire herself, she watched shells burst over Boston and comforted her children more than once when they were roused by the early morning boom of cannon. She was heartened when George Washington arrived to assume command of

BROWN BROTHERS

Left: Saltbox houses belonging to the Adams family.
John Quincy Adams was born
in the cottage at left.

Right: Architect James Hoban's design
for the President's House became a reality
when John and Abigail took up
residence late in 1800.

the American army besieging the British in Boston. Never doubting the fortitude of the patriots, Abigail was typically concerned only with the practical side of the conflict in war-torn New England, observing that, "Courage, I know we have in abundance. . .but powder, where shall we get a sufficient supply?"

While John labored to build a new nation, Abigail did not hesitate to let him know what she thought would make that nation great. Concerning slavery, she wrote, "I wish most sincerely there was not a slave in the province. It always seemed a most iniquitous scheme to me to fight ourselves for what we are robbing the negroes of, who have as good a right to freedom as we have!"

Even more personal were her thoughts on women's rights. "Whilst you are proclaiming peace and good-will to men, emancipating all nations, you insist on retaining absolute power over wives. . . . Remember the ladies and be more generous and favorable to them than your ancestors . . . . Do not put such un-limited power into the hands of the husbands."

John was often amused by his wife's progressive ideas, responding, "You are so saucy!" However, he appreciated her concern for her sex, knowing how much her own intellectual accomplishments had brought to her marriage. She felt:

It is very certain that a well-informed woman, conscious of her nature and dignity, is more capable of performing the relative duties of life, and of engaging and retaining the affections of a man of understanding, than one whose intellectual endowments rise not above the common level.

July 4, 1776, Thomas Jefferson's draft of the Declaration of Independence was adopted in Philadelphia. Abigail stood by while the king's arms were removed from the State House in Boston and burned in State Street. She cheered with the crowds, later writing

feelingly to John, "And all the people shall say Amen."

Like Martha Washington Abigail had hoped that, with the end of the war, she and her husband would no longer be separated. However, when Congress, under the Articles of Confederation, sent John to France as commissioner in 1778, Abigail did not fail to encourage him to discharge his duties to his country. Years later, when she was asked how she bore his long absences, which totaled nearly ten years, she replied, "If I had known, sir, that Mr. Adams could have effected what he has done, I would not only have submitted to the absence I have endured, painful as it has been, but I would not have opposed it, even though three years more should be added to the number (which heaven avert!)."

At last John sent word for Abigail to join him abroad. Traveling with Nabby, she left Thomas in the care of her sister. Her reunion with John would also mean being with John Quincy and Charles again. She had allowed them to accompany their father, yielding to their pleas that such a journey would be invaluable to their education.

In Europe's elegant society the minister's daughter conducted herself with grace and dignity. She learned to respect a culture of which she had been intolerant, struggling to speak French and wrestling with foreign manners and morals. Conquering her misgivings, she came to enjoy the theater and even the ballet. Economizing wherever possible, because the salary the Confederation had voted John was scarcely adequate, Abigail found it hard to circumvent local custom and was sharply criticized for doing her own marketing.

John became the first United States minister to the Court of St. James in 1785. This was an even greater challenge than his assignment in France, for John found it difficult

MARYLAND HISTORICAL SOCIETY

to serve in England on behalf of the new nation. He and Abigail were treated sometimes as country bumpkins and, on other occasions, with open hostility. Abigail's graciousness did much to soothe English feelings, however. John, often blunt and tactless, relied on her charm to soften his own actions.

Anxious to return home, Abigail was delighted when John's years of foreign service drew to a close. They came back to a country newly reunited under the Constitution. George Washington was elected president, with John Adams named vice-president. News of John's election thrilled Abigail. "Sweetly do the birds sing," she wrote.

Periods of ill health had curtailed Abigail's activities somewhat, and she did not follow John to the temporary capital of New York immediately. Once there, however, she took her public responsibilities seriously. Abigail selected one day of the week for her levees, consulting first with Martha Washington, so their choices would not conflict. She and John were comfortable at Richmond Hill, the home selected for the vice-president during the time New York served as capital. However, the seat of government moved before long to Philadelphia, this last transfer in anticipation of its permanent installation in 1800 on the Potomac. Painful bouts of rheumatism finally drove Abigail back to Massachusetts, where she observed with dismay the unpleasant campaign of 1796.

After eight years of service under George Washington, John Adams was elected President of the United States. However, intrigue on the part of Alexander Hamilton had nearly defeated John. In addition, his Federalist leanings were at odds with those of his old friend, Thomas Jefferson, who had been elected vice-president. Jefferson, acknowledging the sorry state of affairs, said as Washington departed, "The President is fortunate to get off just as the bubble is bursting, leaving others to hold the bag."

Domestic squabbles were not the only problems confronting John. Relations with warring France and England were extremely delicate, with hostilities on the high seas involving the United States as well. John gradually became convinced that war with France, no matter how popular among rival political factions, would be disastrous. Fully realizing that his efforts to resolve peacefully America's differences with France might preclude his reelection, John continued to do what he thought best for the nation.

Regardless of their political future, Abigail did her utmost to continue the social traditions established by Martha Washington. Because she had no private income to underwrite her entertaining, Abigail's levees were more modest than Mrs. Washington's. Abigail dressed fashionably in high heels and silk. Not surprisingly, she maintained certain conventions she had been exposed to in Europe. She received guests from a chair, while John, elegant in powdered wig and velvet knee breeches, stood at her shoulder. Critics objected to her chair as "too thronelike," and referred slyly to John as "His Rotundity." Others, however, found gatherings at the Adams' more convivial than those of the Washingtons, and remarked that "Mrs.

15

Sèvres tureen from a set purchased
by John Adams.

WHITE HOUSE HISTORICAL ASSOCIATION

Adams continues the same pleasant person as at Quincy."

As the campaign for the election of 1800 grew more bitter and divisive, Abigail became convinced that John would not win reelection. She was reluctant, therefore, to move into the new President's House when the capital was transferred to Washington, D.C., in the winter of 1800. However, John felt her presence was vital to him. He wrote: "It is fitting and proper that you and I should retire together, and not one before the other."

Her journey to Washington, D.C., was doubly difficult when she learned that her son Charles was near death. Drinking heavily after business reverses, Charles had become desperately ill. Abigail had lost two daughters in infancy, and the knowledge that she would soon lose a son as well opened old wounds.

Abigail's arrival at the President's House, popularly called the Palace, did little to raise her spirits. It was an imposing sandstone mansion, to be sure, but barely six rooms were finished, and the plaster had not yet dried on many of the walls. Her prim housekeeper's soul was appalled at the lack of a fence and a clothesline. Clearly, Abigail saw she must cope with the laundry situation with an eye to saving the washing from the vagaries of stray animals as well as the inquisitive population of the Capital. With typical New England thrift and ingenuity, she solved several problems at once. Commandeering enough wood for fires to help dry the walls of the unfinished Palace, she set up her clothesline in the East Room, the great audience hall. As the plaster dried, so did her wash. Less than delighted with the realities of the President's House, Abigail wisely capitalized on its historical significance. "This house," she acknowledged, "is built for ages to come."

Abigail endeavored to establish a dignified social salon in the new capital, regardless of how short her stay there. Her greatest efforts went toward organizing the first full-dress reception held in the President's House on New Year's Day 1801. With this affair, society in Washington, D.C., was launched.

The Inauguration of Thomas Jefferson on March 4, 1801, brought to a close the public lives of John and Abigail Adams. Saddened by John's failure to win reelection, they retired to their Massachusetts farm. Abigail felt history would vindicate her husband's judgment on foreign affairs, unpopular though they may have been during his lifetime. She concluded, "I leave to posterity to reflect upon the times past; and I leave them characters to contemplate." She did indeed. In 1825, seven years after her death, her son John Quincy Adams became the sixth President of the United States.

Abigail would have been amused that another president, Harry Truman, chief executive nearly a century and a half after John Adams, said of her, "She would have made a better president than her husband." Her intellect and interest in current affairs were remarkable for a woman of her era, but she did not question her husband's superior ability. A thoroughly devoted couple, Abigail could not have refrained from giving John advice, nor would he have wished her to.

Her unselfish patriotism had helped launch the United States of America, and her influence, with John's, was intricately woven into the fabric of our emerging nation. Abigail's legacy is one of profound moral conviction, much of which she instilled in her son, John Quincy, reminding him that, "these are the times in which a genius would wish to live. It is not in the still calm of life or the repose of a pacific station, that great characters are formed . . . . The habits of a vigorous mind are formed in contending with difficulties. . . . Great necessities call out great virtues."

# 3
# Martha Jefferson

## Never to be First Lady*

Thomas Jefferson moved into the President's House in 1801, bringing with him that spring only a distant memory of the woman who would have been his First Lady. He never revealed his wife's letters, and no portrait of her is known to have survived. Martha Jefferson, with four of their six children, lay lost to history in the family graveyard at Monticello.

Martha Wayles Skelton had been "the fair one" Thomas had courted in 1771. She was the widow of Bathurst Skelton (a contemporary of Jefferson), who died when Martha was nineteen. The lovely, auburn-haired widow had many suitors, but she loved the tall, brilliant man from Monticello. Jefferson offered himself to Martha as a husband and as guardian of her small son, but the sudden death of the child postponed wedding plans for an interval of mourning.

Envisioning a magnificent home for them at Monticello, Jefferson pointed out to his fiancée that the small brick pavilion currently comprising the estate would soon be merely the extension of an exquisite house. Optimistically ordering furnishings for this mansion, Jefferson first provided for Martha's and his own love of music. Commissioning a "forte-piano," he insisted the instrument be "very handsome and worthy the acceptance of a lady for whom I intend it." Martha was already accomplished at spinet and harpsichord, while Jefferson's spirited fiddling sparked their courting hours.

They were married New Year's Day 1772 at Martha's father's home, with traditional Virginia wedding festivities continuing for weeks. At last the newlyweds left on a wedding journey that was destined to become part of the romantic legend of Monticello. Caught in a biting snowstorm, heavy drifts forced them to abandon their carriage some eight miles from home. Struggling up the treacherous mountain on horseback, they arrived late at night at the little brick "Honeymoon Cottage." Reluctant to awaken anyone to set the fires, the half-frozen, hungry newlyweds chased the "horrible dreariness" with "song and merriment and laughter."

Their marriage held little more laughter, however. During the next ten years, Martha gave birth to six children, four of whom died in infancy. Always delicate, Martha's health was totally broken by childbearing and the emotional ravages of her babies' deaths. Only two daughters, Patsy and Maria, lived.

Despite the acclaim he had received as author of the Declaration of Independence, Jefferson curtailed many of his political activities to remain with Martha. Refusing an appointment as commissioner to France, he served instead in Virginia's House of Delegates, and, later, as governor. They lived for a time at the Governor's Palace in Williamsburg, but moved to Richmond when the government was transferred there. Warned of approaching British troops, Martha and her five-week-old baby fled the city. The infant died shortly afterward, and Martha, grieving, became pregnant once more. She never recovered from this last confinement, and Thomas, realizing she had not long to live, remained at her side at Monticello.

There, the woman admired as his "mild and amiable wife," died September 6, 1782. Little Patsy never forgot the depth of her father's despair that day, recalling "The violence of his emotion, when...I entered his room by night, to this day I dare not describe to myself."

Jefferson had written of his beloved Martha "In every scheme of happiness she is placed in the foreground of the picture, as the principal figure. Take that away, and there is no picture for me." He never remarried, leaving the duties of First Lady to his daughter, Patsy Jefferson Randolph, and Dolley Madison, wife of his Secretary of State.

* No known portrait exists.

17

# 4
# Dolley Madison

## Hostess to the Nation

The election of James Madison in 1809 brought new social dimensions to the presidency. Declaring "The nation's guests are my guests," his blooming, radiant Dolley presided through eight years of unparalleled hospitality in the President's House.

Martha Washington knew and admired Dolley Madison, whose real name was indeed Dolley, not as some thought, Dorothea. Like Martha, Dolley had been left a young widow. Her husband, John Todd, a Quaker lawyer, and infant son, William, had died in the Philadelphia yellow fever epidemic of 1793. With Payne, her surviving son, Dolley returned to the Capital after her own recovery.

The handsome widow Todd was fortunate to have many friends in the Capital, including George and Martha Washington. Still in mourning, she circumspectly avoided public amusements, but continued her custom of paying and receiving daily social calls. Marketing in town, wearing a simple Quaker bonnet and graceful gray dress, she was a charming contrast to mincing, modish ladies. Companions noticed that "gentlemen would station themselves where they could see her pass," although Dolley herself was disbelieving when friends told her she attracted considerable attention.

One bystander was sufficiently impressed with the amiable widow to seek an introduction. He was James Madison, the Virginian known for his brilliant work in the framing of the Constitution. Now serving in the House of Representatives, James, at forty-three, was thought to be a confirmed bachelor. Regardless, one brief glimpse of Dolley, along with what he knew of her background, was nearly enough to convince him she was the woman he had sought for so long.

Many of Dolley's relatives, like his own, were well-known Virginians. Her reputation was particularly fine because, although certain of her would-be suitors were government officials, she did not exchange political gossip. Shortly after he had been intrigued by the appearance of Mrs. Todd, James asked Senator Aaron Burr, one of her admirers, to arrange an introduction. The maneuver completely outflanked Burr, for he could not refuse Madison's request without prematurely declaring his own intentions.

Flustered by news that James Madison wanted to meet her, Dolley sought moral support from a friend, writing, "Thou must come to me at once. Burr says the Great Little Madison has asked to be brought to me this evening." Despite her initial nervousness, the meeting was a success. Shortly afterward, Madison confessed he had fallen in love with her and asked Dolley to marry him.

Rumors of their romance swept Philadelphia. Delighted, Martha Washington advised Dolley, "He will make thee a good husband, and all the better for being so much older. We both approve of it; the esteem and friendship between my husband and Mr. Madison is very great, and we would wish thee to be happy." Despite the fact that marriage to James would mean expulsion from the Quaker meeting, Dolley accepted his proposal. On her wedding day, September 15, 1794, she wrote, "In the course of this day I give my hand to the man of all others I most admire."

The newlyweds were popular guests in the Capital, and their own open-house entertaining was an immediate success. Dolley's guest lists were always politically impartial, and politics were taboo at her gatherings. Even John Adams, increasingly at odds with James, expressed his approval of Dolley.

With the retirement of George Washington, James, too, left public life. Choosing not to run for reelection, he anticipated peaceful years as a country squire. Dolley, who had lived as a child on a Virginia farm, was deeply content to move to Montpelier, the

Madison homestead. They visited Thomas Jefferson at nearby Monticello often, listening attentively to his comments on current events. The vice-president drew his best friend into deep political discussions, making it increasingly difficult for James to remain aloof from public affairs. Returning before long to the state legislature, Madison renewed his political affiliations, campaigning vigorously in support of Republican policies.

The death of George Washington in 1799 brought James and Dolley together with Thomas Jefferson at Mount Vernon, where they paid their respects to Martha Washington. The passing of the great man made the survival of the nation he had served so well seem vitally important. Dolley knew Jefferson would challenge John Adams in the coming elections, and suspected that a Republican victory would return James to government service in the new capital on the banks of the Potomac.

When Thomas Jefferson and Aaron Burr unexpectedly tied for the presidency in 1800, the Madisons anxiously awaited the results of balloting in the House of Representatives. They rejoiced at word of Jefferson's victory and were not surprised when a message from the president-elect requested James to serve as Secretary of State. Certain James would respond to the appeal of his friend, Dolley knew that her future, too, lay in Washington.

The woman who would exert a profound influence on the new capital arrived there May 1, 1802. Jefferson had insisted that the Madisons join him at the Palace, and arrange for their own lodgings later on. It had been easy for Dolley to sympathize with Abigail Adams' plight, struggling to make a home of the huge, unfinished mansion. However, now decorated with Jefferson's lovely Monticello furnishings, the Executive Mansion was very attractive.

Just three weeks after her arrival in Wash-

PAINTING ATTRIBUTED TO BASS OTIS, NEW-YORK HISTORICAL SOCIETY

ington, Jefferson called upon Dolley to assist him with social functions, asking that she dine with him to "take care of female friends expected." Her splendid efforts on his behalf affirmed his selection of her as his official hostess. Occasionally, Jefferson's daughter, Patsy, or other cabinet members' wives did the honors, but Dolley's unequaled charm and capability made her the President's favorite. In her own home, Dolley renewed her policy of non-partisan entertaining. The Madisons turned their house on F Street into a convivial headquarters for important men and their families. Before long, Mrs. Madison was recognized as a peerless social leader. The weekly assemblies she co-sponsored soon rivaled the long-established dances of Georgetown, Alexandria and Annapolis. Mrs. Madison had somehow managed to create society where there had been none,

19

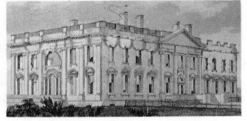

LIBRARY OF CONGRESS

Blackened shell of the White House after the British burned it in 1814.

and congressmen and senators began leaving the suburbs, taking up residence in Washington, D.C.

Political intrigue continued to intrude on social relationships. Jefferson's republican code of manners sometimes caused difficulties. Mrs. Merry, wife of the English ambassador, was insulted when Jefferson took Dolley's arm, instead of her own, to lead his guests in to dinner one evening. Noticing Mrs. Merry's displeasure, Dolley tried to defer to her, but Jefferson ignored Dolley's gesture, sweeping her along with him. But Washington's reputation was enhanced, rather than hurt, when social incidents with international repercussions occurred. Soon a recognized city of fashion, the Capital flourished.

Since Jefferson had restricted presidential open houses to New Year's Day and the 4th of July, the scene of greatest social activity in Washington was the home of the Secretary of State. Mrs. Madison's receptions were deservedly memorable. She prepared gift lotteries for her guests, with prizes for everyone, win or lose. She did not entertain in the "punch and cake" tradition of the Continent, but offered her guests a bountiful board, complemented by her husband's excellent wines. The reputation of her table was such that Mrs. Merry, still angry with the Jefferson administration, unkindly criticized its abundance. Undaunted, Dolley commented simply, "The profusion of my table so repugnant to foreign customs arises from the happy circumstances of abundance and prosperity in our country."

The Quaker society Dolley had known which encouraged conversation as the only social diversion now served her well. Dolley's remarkable memory for names and faces was a priceless asset, enabling her to chat easily with each guest, often picking up the thread of conversation where they had dropped it at their last meeting. Frequently she

eased awkward moments by extending her enameled snuff box, inviting friends to join her in a pinch of her favorite blend.

Nearing the end of his eight years in office, Jefferson adamantly rejected a third term. Although James was his obvious choice as successor, opposing party factions made the campaign unpleasant. Certain James would win, Dolley's confidence in her husband was rewarded when the electoral votes were counted, and James Madison was declared fourth President of the United States.

Shimmering in pale yellow satin, Dolley greeted hundreds of well-wishers at the nation's first Inaugural Ball. As Jefferson's hostess, she had already earned the respect of the Capital. As First Lady in her own right, she won the admiration and lasting affection of the entire nation.

Dolley reinstated diplomatic etiquette, observing the order of precedence, while maintaining the friendly, diplomatic approach Jefferson had favored. She carried on her customary social calls, feeling she should go to the public in the same spirit that the public came to her. The Wednesday levee was revived, and, in addition, she planned weekly state dinners, special affairs for foreign dignitaries, and "dove parties" for the cabinet wives. For the first time since the birth of the republic, men and women of the country's first families could participate in a society worthy of their attention.

The probability of war with England overshadowed the gaiety in the Capital, however. As James Madison's first term ended, the Federalists boycotted Dolley's receptions, hoping to undermine his popularity and defeat his bid for reelection. They were thwarted by his victory, however, and a jubilant Dolley set the stage for their continued occupancy of the Palace. New Year's Day 1813 the Executive Mansion stood open to everyone who chose to come.

Dolley Madison cup and saucer made by
Dagoty of Paris.

WHITE HOUSE HISTORICAL ASSOCIATION

War with England became a reality in June, and as months passed, Dolley heard persistent hints that the British fleet anchored offshore planned an invasion of Washington. Finally, with the arrival of reinforcements, the enemy made its move. The morning of August 24, 1814, fighting began in nearby Bladensburg. James rushed there with his advisors, while Dolley remained at the Palace.

Word that the American troops had been routed dismayed Dolley, but she refused to flee, stoutly remaining calm while she packed as many state valuables as possible. "I have pressed as many cabinet papers into trunks as to fill one carriage," she noted. "Our private property must be sacrificed." Ignoring her famous, extensive wardrobe, Dolley supervised the removal of vital documents and other property of the nation.

Washington had become a city of refugees, all rushing out of town. Even the hundred soldiers left to stand guard had gone, leaving the Capital defenseless. Messengers arrived, confirming the American defeat at Bladensburg. Still, Dolley stood firm, maintaining that one more treasure be preserved. "I insist on waiting until the large picture of George Washington is secured, and it requires to be unscrewed from the wall. This process was found too tedious for these perilous moments; I have ordered the frame to be broken and the canvas taken out. . . ."

At all costs, Dolley was determined to keep the British from seizing the priceless symbols of American government, advising her envoys in event of capture to "destroy the portrait of General Washington, the eagles which ornament the dining room, and the four cases of papers."

Maintaining that she was "so unfeminine as to be free from fear," Dolley confessed she was "willing to remain in the Castle! If I could have had a cannon through every window; but, alas, those who should have placed them fled before me, and my whole heart mourned for my country."

No longer able to ignore the warning of the British commander, who threatened to burn the Palace over her head if she remained, Dolley left at last. In the terror-filled days that followed, she became a fugitive, frequently without shelter when citizens closed their homes to her. Some feared for their own safety if her whereabouts were discovered, while others, blaming James for the defeat at Bladensburg, took their revenge on Dolley.

News that the British had been driven back to their ships by a violent storm immediately brought James back to Washington, sending word for Dolley to join him. Disguised as a poor country woman, she had ridden some distance from the Capital. The moment her husband's message reached her, she headed back to Washington.

The British had indeed made their threatened "bow in Mrs. Madison's drawing room." The stone walls of the mansion were scarred and black, its interior utterly destroyed. Grief-stricken, Dolley saw the ruins of the Capitol and Hall of Representatives. The storm had saved the Treasury building, however, and the Post and Patents office had been spared.

Its losses were great, but Washington had not been totally leveled. James conducted business from the saddle while Dolley set up housekeeping in their old house on F Street. Soon, they moved to the Octagon, a lovely home left intact. Despite pressures to remove the capital once more to Philadelphia, the President and his wife left no doubt that Washington would not be abandoned. The British fleet repulsed at Baltimore had apparently sailed away and the Madisons' exemplary behavior soon reinstated them in public affection. "Peace Winter" came at last, following acceptance of the Treaty of Ghent

21

and Andrew Jackson's decisive victory at New Orleans. Pleased with this happy ending to his administration, James applauded the election of James Monroe, considering his friend's victory a vote of confidence for himself as well.

In retirement at Montpelier, James devoted his final years to compiling his notes of the Constitutional Convention. Aware of their value, he hoped Dolley would be provided for by their sale. Montpelier no longer supported itself, and the excesses of his stepson, Payne Todd, were a constant drain on Madison's reserves.

Despite failing health, the aging statesman worked long hours on his manuscript. Finally, nearly blind, and crippled with rheumatism, he relied on Dolley's eyes and hands to finish his work. When he died in 1836, President Andrew Jackson, as a testimonial of respect for her person and public character, conferred upon Dolley the franking privilege and a seat on the floor of the House of Representatives.

The responsibility for completing her husband's papers on the Constitution was Dolley's alone. Continuing despite her grief, she felt "The best return I can make for the sympathy of my country is to fulfill the sacred trust his confidence reposed in me, that of placing before it and the world what his pen prepared for their use." She discharged her responsibility well. Congress purchased the first half of the Madison papers in September, and Dolley returned to Washington again.

Approaching the President's House, she saw that the sooty evidence of the British invasion had been completely erased. Snowy paint disguised the smoke-blackened walls. The Capital extended a warm welcome to its former First Lady, receiving her quickly as its favorite hostess, for widowers Andrew Jackson and Martin Van Buren had brought no wives with them to the White House.

But as years passed Dolley confronted the financial problems James had feared would overwhelm her. Having sold all of Montpelier except the family cemetery, she relied on the sale of the remaining Madison papers to insure her future.

The Senate authorized their purchase, but the House failed to take prompt action, leaving Dolley on the verge of poverty. Her friends did not desert her in this time of difficulty, bringing laden market baskets when they came to call and inviting her for extended visits at their homes. She remained the *grande dame* of Washington, honored by succeeding administrations. The Tylers kept a place for her in their carriage on all official occasions, and her advice was sought on important social matters. A friend recalled, "When I knew her in after life, widowed, poor, and without prestige of station, I found her the same goodnatured, kindhearted, considerate, stately person that she had been in the hey-day of her fortunes." Another confirmed that "she was the only one who exercised as much social sway in official life after her retirement from the White House as she did before."

Dolley's eightieth birthday finally stirred Congress to favorable action on the remaining Madison papers. At last, with her future secure, Dolley found peace and pleasure once more in her beloved Washington.

The death of Dolley Madison on July 12, 1849, brought President Zachary Taylor and countless government officials, past and present, together in extraordinary mourning for an extraordinary woman. She had been First Lady in deed as well as name, bringing elevating manners and traditions to the new democratic society. Dolley had served the nation with honor and affection, giving much of herself to ensure the permanence of Washington. She holds a place in history not only as a hostess, but as a patriot.

# 5
## Elizabeth Monroe

### Formal First Lady

Elizabeth Monroe had no desire to rival Dolley Madison's formidable record as the nation's hostess. Flourishing local society no longer needed the nurturing of the First Lady, and Elizabeth would direct her energies instead toward improving America's diplomatic stature. Declaring she was decidedly "not at home" for social purposes at her house on I Street following the inauguration of her husband in 1817, she further announced that she would call on no one, abandoning Mrs. Madison's custom.

President Monroe completely supported his wife's position. He himself would receive foreign ministers only by appointment or at official dinners, achieving the same "form and ceremony" to which American ministers were subjected in foreign courts. He and Elizabeth were completely familiar with European traditions, having served many years abroad. They favored encouraging similar formality at White House functions, particularly as a means of winning greater respect from foreign dignitaries.

James had confidence in his wife's social judgments. The daughter of a former British army officer, she had been launched in fashionable New York society before their marriage. Then, too, she had acquitted herself admirably abroad. Her beauty and refinement had, in fact, probably attracted him to her. Slender, auburn-haired Elizabeth Kortright caught and quickly held the attention of James Monroe, then representing Virginia in the Continental Congress. James called their marriage in February 1786, "the most interesting connection in human life." Delighted with his bride, he told Thomas Jefferson that he must "relinquish all other objects not connected with her." Urging another friend, James Madison, to visit them in Fredericksburg, Virginia, where he had located his law office, Monroe added "I will present you to a young lady who will be adopted a citizen of Virginia in the course of this week."

The Monroes' horizons stretched far beyond their home state. Politics beckoned, and the young lawyer inched toward a career in public service. President Washington appointed him minister to France in 1794, and he later served four terms as governor of Virginia. Returning to Europe in 1803, he spent four years as Jefferson's emissary to France, England and Spain.

Particularly admired in France as "la belle Américaine," Elizabeth's affinity for French culture added to her popularity. Consequently, James enlisted her aid in a delicate matter of diplomacy. Madame Lafayette had been imprisoned and was reportedly facing the guillotine. Political considerations precluded Monroe's direct intervention, but he reasoned that a display of public sentiment on her behalf might sway the authorities. Dispatching Elizabeth to the prison, he hoped his wife's

PAINTING BY EBEN COMINS, WHITE HOUSE COLLECTION

Bronze-doré clock with figurine of Hannibal, one of the treasured Monroe purchases.

WHITE HOUSE HISTORICAL ASSOCIATION

demonstration of concern for Madame Lafayette might lead to her release. Elizabeth's mission succeeded, for soon after her emotion-charged meeting with the wife of the Marquis at the gate of Le Plessis prison, Madame Lafayette was freed.

Elizabeth shared defeat as well as triumph with her husband. James was recalled once for failing to negotiate an acceptable treaty, and, while in England, was criticized for being overly sympathetic to the French. In addition, he and Elizabeth were snubbed in London in retaliation for Jefferson's neglect of haughty Mrs. Merry, wife of the English ambassador.

It should have come as no surprise, therefore, that Elizabeth would countenance no breach of diplomatic etiquette during her husband's presidency. Frequent illness, however, made it impossible for her to attend and supervise all official functions. Long hours in her green cambric-shrouded bedroom kept her far removed from the social scene at these times.

Eliza Monroe Hay, Elizabeth and James Monroe's married daughter, served as White House hostess when her mother was ailing. Lacking Elizabeth's gentle charm, Eliza drew criticism and resentment for her social dictums. It was she who announced that the marriage of her younger sister, Maria, first daughter of a president to marry in the White House, would be "New York style," very small, very quiet. Instead, pretty, popular Maria and her husband, Samuel Lawrence Gouverneur, were feted after their honeymoon. Mrs. Monroe made no attempt to interfere with Eliza's plans despite Maria's pleas. Either her illnesses were more debilitating than the public knew, or she herself approved of the modest wedding arrangements.

When her health permitted and despite her personal inclination, Elizabeth Monroe endeavored to fulfill the many obligations thrust upon her as First Lady. Limiting her entertaining to formal occasions, she gave twice-monthly receptions during the social season, receiving diplomats and ranking officials a half hour before other guests.

Still a beauty, she appeared regal in her favorite black velvet, ostrich plumes quivering in carefully dressed hair. Despite her reputation for snobbishness, she saw that a delegation of Plains Indians were received with pomp and ceremony in 1821. Ladies of the Capital, who had boycotted her receptions for a time in protest of what they felt was unnecessary formality, finally abandoned this futile expression of their feelings. By her last White House entertainment in the winter of 1825, Elizabeth even won grudging admiration from an observer who noted, "Mrs. Monroe's manner is very gracious and she is a regal-looking lady .... Though no longer young, she is still a very handsome woman."

It was generally acknowledged, after all, that Elizabeth's parties, against the background of the newly decorated White House, made up in setting what they lacked in spontaneity. The Executive Mansion, furnished by the Monroes with a breathtaking collection of French imports, had reopened in the fall of 1817.

The nickname, "White House," which had cropped up occasionally in reference to the Executive Mansion even when it was most commonly known as the Palace, or President's House, suddenly seemed awesomely appropriate. Its original creamy sandstone walls, disfigured by British torches, had been painted a splendid, gleaming white.

Elizabeth Monroe herself was responsible for salvaging some of the very few souvenirs of Dolley Madison's White House trappings. Investigating the rubble outside the mansion, Elizabeth retrieved pieces of Dolley's celebrated looking glasses and had them made into small stand-mirrors. To refurnish the

Pier table and armchair by Bellangé,
part of the furnishings ordered from France
during the Monroe administration.

BOTH: WHITE HOUSE HISTORICAL ASSOCIATION

White House, James and Elizabeth used their own furniture chiefly in their private quarters, purchasing fine new pieces for those rooms intended for official entertaining.

Elizabeth's first-floor oval reception room, ablaze in crimson and gold, was even more splendid than the First Lady had anticipated. The French craftsman who had received the order for its varnished mahogany chairs, gilded the furniture instead, considering the gold finish more appropriate for a head of state. Criticism of the Monroe purchases as "overfine" dimmed in the undeniable beauty of their selections. Elizabeth herself supervised the making of thousands of candles to fill her exquisite bronze-and-crystal chandeliers, and the imposing many-branched canddelabra. Her guests admired the pier table in the oval room, checking and adjusting their skirts in its mirrored base, which reflected the soft hues of an Aubusson carpet. The unique mirrored centerpiece for the state

dining room adapted itself to candles, flowers, or fruit, and was something of a sensation. The Monroes' choices endured even the test of time, for today their collection of bronze-doré, the pier table and many other pieces of furniture, clocks and bric-a-brac survive as White House treasures.

Aloof, serenely removed from politics, Elizabeth cultivated few friendships, content with her husband's and daughters' company. She left a firm social order for her successors, at the same time providing them with a welcome precedent for establishing their own routines. More important, perhaps, was the abiding love and support she gave James until her death in 1830. Then, brokenhearted, he impressed a friend with his "touching grief. . .on the morning of Mrs. Monroe's death, when he sent for me to go to his room, and with trembling frame and streaming eyes spoke of the long years they had spent happily together."

25

# 6
## Louisa Adams

### Cultured First Lady

PAINTING BY GILBERT STUART, WHITE HOUSE COLLECTION

"Belles and matrons, maids and madams, All are gone to Mrs. Adams'." Recalling the gay doggerel that had immortalized her 1817 reception for Andrew Jackson, Louisa Adams realized her husband's Inaugural Ball, eight years later, was by comparison a lackluster affair. She knew John Quincy's victory in the election of 1824 was bittersweet at best, for Jackson, their one-time friend, had garnered more notes than John. Lacking a majority, however, the general had lost the election in the House of Representatives when minority candidate Henry Clay threw his support to Adams.

Sensitive to the ironies of her husband's election, Louisa declined to flaunt her own new position. She was not unhappy that ailing Elizabeth Monroe had asked to postpone her departure from the White House for a few weeks. Unawed by the presidency, Louisa's daily habits would undergo little change.

Years after his son's marriage, John Adams had remarked that John Quincy's "choice of a wife was the wisest choice of his whole career." However, when Louisa and John were wed in 1797, neither John nor Abigail Adams had met their son's bride. John Quincy was in diplomatic service abroad, and, learning of his engagement, Abigail confessed herself patriotic enough to hope the "Siren" would be half American. Happily, Louisa Catherine Johnson was the daughter of an Englishwoman and a Maryland importer serving in London as American consul. John's brother Thomas sang her praises from London. He told his mother that "John Quincy is very happy and doubtless will remain so, for the young lady . . .is indeed a most lovely woman, and in my opinion worthy in every respect of the man for whom she has. . .renounced father and mother, kindred and country, to unite her destinies with his." Reassured, Abigail advised John Quincy to "marry the lady .give my love to her and tell her I consider her already as my daughter, and, as she made England delightful to you I hope she will every other country."

Louisa was grateful for the scope of her mother-in-law's good wishes. John Quincy would serve in Prussia, the Netherlands, England and even Russia. Her facility with several languages delighted her husband, as did her fondness for reading the *Dialogues of Plato* to their sons in original Greek. She played both harp and spinet, and frequently sang in the evenings to her own accompaniment. An avid reader, she devoured the classics, but confessed the "modern" philosophers, such as Locke and Hume, either puzzled or disgusted her.

She had need of her books and music when John's appointment as minister to Russia took them far from home and friends. At the end of five years, John was sent to the Ghent peace conference, while Louisa stayed

26

Louisa Adams traveled from St. Petersburg across war-ravaged Europe to rejoin her husband in Paris.

behind. Her only companion was her small son Charles, for his brothers, John and George, were in America. At last, his treaty signed, John Quincy sent word for Louisa to meet him in Paris. For nearly two months, she and Charles traveled across war-ravaged Europe, Louisa confessing her "whole heart was filled with unspeakable terrors for the safety of the child." At the mercy of highwaymen and deserters, her Russian carriage frequently mistaken for an advance guard of Cossacks, Louisa "jolted over hills, through swamps and holes, and into valleys into which no carriage had surely ever passed before."

Reunited at last, John and Louisa left for England, where John was to serve at the Court of St. James. It was difficult to thaw diplomatic relationships chilled by the War of 1812, but Louisa, part English, emerged as a distinct asset to John Quincy. His accomplishments abroad led to his appointment as President Monroe's Secretary of State, and in 1817, after an absence of many years, John and Louisa returned to America.

In Washington, surrounded once more by her sons, Louisa became a sought-after hostess. Like Dolley Madison, she attempted to divorce politics from social gatherings. Her son recalled, "During the eight years in which Mrs. Adams presided in the house of the Secretary of State, no exclusions were made in her invitations, merely on account of any real or imagined political hostility." However, as the election of 1828 approached, Charles further noted that "the violence of partisan warfare began to manifest its usual bad effects, and Mrs. Adams decided to adopt habits of greater seclusion."

John Quincy's far from decisive victory, therefore, and the lingering unpleasantness, made Louisa value her privacy still more. Alarmed, too, by Louisa's obviously failing health, John encouraged her quiet domesticity. She enjoyed peaceful evenings with him, reading, composing French verse, or peering at the stars through the telescope he had installed on the White House roof.

Although she was not always well, Louisa continued her custom of Tuesday evening drawing rooms, and entertained beautifully whenever occasion demanded. She honored the Marquis de Lafayette on his sixty-eighth birthday, and in 1828 planned the first wedding of a president's son to take place in the White House. Silken-gloved and stylish at all public appearances, she smiled even when the political tide was turning against her husband. Critics, however, mocked her behavior in defeat as "a brilliant masquerade dress of social, gay, frank, cordial manners."

Privately, John and Louisa were depressed and disheartened at his failure to win re-election. New Year's Day 1829 John confessed, "The year begins in gloom. My wife had a sleepless and painful night." Personal tragedy added to their sorrows when they lost their eldest son, George.

Many years earlier, in 1819, Louisa had expressed her faith in the ultimate good of the American people, commenting they "may often be deceived for a time. . .but they will never be deceived for long. Though they may, in a moment of excitement, sanction an injustice toward an old and faithful servant, they appreciate his worth." In the case of her husband, her words were prophetic. The people of Massachusetts refused to allow John Quincy to retire, sending him back to Washington as a congressman. In the ensuing seventeen years, Louisa saw John emerge as "Old Man Eloquent," tirelessly fighting slavery. She stood by at his death in the Speaker's Room of the Capitol in 1848.

Before her own death in 1852, her grandson, Henry Adams, described his adored grandmother as "singularly peaceful, a vision of silver gray, an exotic, like her Sèvres china; an object of deference to everyone."

27

# 7
# Rachel Jackson

PAINTING BY HOWARD CHANDLER CHRISTY, WHITE HOUSE COLLECTION

## Pursued by Scandal

Andrew Jackson strode grimly to the Capitol for his Inauguration in March 1829, a wide mourning band circling his sleeve. His Rachel, who should have been beside him, lay in a fresh grave at the Hermitage, swathed in the lavish satin folds of her white Inaugural gown. At her funeral, convinced that "slanderous tongues" had caused her fatal heart attack, Jackson declared "In the presence of this dead saint I can and do forgive my enemies. But those vile wretches who have slandered her must look to God for mercy."

It was true that scandal had pursued Rachel most of her life and that she had endured more than her share of vilification. Quick to defend her reputation, Jackson had fought many duels, killing one man and bearing in his own body two bullets never removed.

Born in Virginia, where her father, Colonel John Donelson, had served in the House of Burgesses, Rachel had moved with her family to the new settlements in Tennessee and later to Kentucky. Here on the frontier she met Captain Lewis Robards whom she married at the age of seventeen in 1784. Her marriage was a nightmare almost from the start, for Robards was notoriously unfaithful, abusive and drunken. In 1788 no longer able to bear him, she fled to her widowed mother's place in Nashville.

There she met Andrew Jackson, a gaunt, red-haired lawyer who had taken lodgings at her mother's boardinghouse. She returned to Kentucky with Robards, however, when he came to claim her. In 1790, when their domestic relations had deteriorated to the point where her family feared for her safety, Andrew brought her back to Nashville. A year later, believing that Robards had secured a divorce, Jackson and Rachel were married. They were unaware that the legislature had merely granted Robards permission to sue for divorce and had not actually granted a decree. Vengefully waiting to obtain a divorce until September 1793, Robards did so on the grounds that Rachel "doth still live in adultery with another man."

Although they were married in a second ceremony Jackson never forgave himself for not having personally verified Robards' first divorce petition. As his military life was superseded by a political one, the hero of the Battle of New Orleans was unable to prevent his detractors from dragging Rachel's matrimonial record before the public.

Shamed and saddened by the cruel invectives, Rachel turned to her church for comfort. Those who knew her reputation for charity and kindness shared her sorrow. She was "Aunt Rachel" to scores of children, having none of her own until she legally adopted one nephew and gave a permanent home to another. Meanwhile, the slender beauty had become "a coarse-looking, stout, little old woman." But Jackson's feelings for Rachel were unchanged, an observer noting, "The General always treated her as if she were his pride and glory."

Jackson's election in 1828 brought unwanted fame to Rachel. "I had rather be a door-keeper in the house of God than to live in that palace," she said prophetically, for she did not survive to preside in the White House. Apparently malicious gossip she had overheard in Nashville, where she had gone for a fitting for her Inaugural gown, triggered her collapse. She died in late December 1828; the years of gossip, slander and anxiety had taken their toll. Treasuring her memory, Andrew wore Rachel's ivory miniature around his neck until his own death in 1845.

# 8

# Hannah Van Buren

LIBRARY OF CONGRESS

## "Little Van's" Lady

Widower Martin Van Buren, unlike Andrew Jackson, did not bring fresh grief and bitterness with him to the White House in 1837. His Hannah had been dead for nearly twenty years and the President's memory of her was unclouded by the scandal and heartbreak Rachel Jackson had suffered. Nor had Hannah's death left him totally alone, for four handsome sons shared his loss.

Although Martin and Hannah Hoes Van Buren had been married only twelve years, they had pledged themselves to one another when they were very young. Raised in the Dutch settlement of Kinderhook, New York, east of the Hudson, they had postponed their marriage until Matt had established himself as an attorney. Her energetic, sunny beau, lacking formal schooling, had apprenticed himself at the age of fourteen to a lawyer for whom he set fires and swept floors in exchange for instruction.

Matt progressed rapidly, and Hannah was not surprised to learn that at seventeen he had won his first case and had attracted the attention of some prominent politicians. In 1801 he went to far-off Manhattan to finish his clerkship, while Hannah waited in Kinderhook, sewing for her dowry and giving much of her time to church work.

The polished attorney who returned to sleepy Kinderhook several years later had not forgotten his faithful Dutch sweetheart. "Little Van" was a small man but Hannah, a fragile delft figurine, was smaller still. They were married in February 1807, after Matt was sworn in as counselor to the state supreme court. The newlyweds set up housekeeping in Kinderhook but Matt's blossoming career soon took them to Hudson and eventually to Albany. As state senator and as New York State attorney general, Matt grew wealthy and influential, but more and more treasured his wife, "Jannetje," and their tranquil home. There, in their house on Columbia Street, he and Hannah chattered cheerfully in Dutch.

Deeply religious, Hannah's devotion to her church was a source of both strength and pleasure. Joining the Presbyterian Church in Albany where there were no Dutch Reformed congregations, Hannah concerned herself with the church's charitable works. Her consideration for the needy was so great that it was said the poor knew her better than anyone outside her own family.

At first the move to the state capital appeared to be beneficial. Then Matt realized that the rosy young woman who had so loved sleigh riding and skating with him on the frozen Hudson near Kinderhook had become weak and ill. During their first winter in Albany temperatures had dropped to 24 and 32 degrees below zero and Hannah had developed a severe cough and chronic cold. Warm spring and summer weather did nothing to improve her condition, and by September it was clear she had tuberculosis and would never regain her strength. She died in February 1819, having called her sons to her some hours before, and with "utmost composure bade them farewell." Even in death she demonstrated her dedication to the poor, requesting that the customary mourning scarves be eliminated at her funeral and the money for that purpose be given to charity.

Martin Van Buren never remarried; mourning their loss together, he and his sons became unusually close, even after the boys were grown. It was his eldest son, Abraham, who provided the White House with a ravishing hostess when he married Angelica Singleton, a young relative of Dolley Madison.

29

# 9
## Anna Harrison

BENJAMIN HARRISON HOME

### Frontier Matriarch

"I wish my husband's friends had left him where he is, happy and contented in retirement," Anna Harrison said, unimpressed with William Henry's victory over Martin Van Buren in the 1840 election. The new First Lady, a seasoned frontierswoman in her mid-sixties, was ill for one of the few times in her life. Having recently lost a grown son and besieged in recent months by her husband's favor-seeking cronies, she was too sick to travel with "Old Tippecanoe" to Washington.

Recuperating at home on the Ohio frontier, Anna anticipated exciting reports of the Inaugural festivities. Instead, shocking news that her husband lay seriously ill was followed quickly by word of his death. The elaborate state funeral of the first president to die in office had been held without his widow on April 7. Grief-stricken, Anna realized there was nothing more she could do for her beloved William than receive his body.

It was an unspeakably sad homecoming for the hearty warrior who had had so many rousing welcomes from his family in the past. Having promised to support his slight, dimpled bride "with my sword and my good right arm," Harrison had fought the Indians at Tippecanoe and the British at Detroit. Serving in Congress and as minister to Colombia, he left behind a spirited woman of obvious courage who faced the wilderness "unguarded."

Peril was no stranger to Anna, though the Indians that terrorized her in Ohio were not the same enemy she had feared as a child. In 1779, when she was just four years old, a skirmish broke out between the Redcoats and the Continental Army near her Morristown, New Jersey, home. Her father, widower Judge Symmes, smuggled Anna out from behind enemy lines, taking her to be with her grandparents. There, on Long Island, she grew into a beautiful young woman, well-educated for her day, having attended nearby Clinton Academy and, later, Miss Graham's Boarding School in New York.

Fashionable city life claimed her for only a short time. At nineteen Anna joined her father in a raw settlement of the Northwest Territory. A whirlwind romance with young Captain Harrison, on duty at nearby Fort Washington, first pleased then dismayed Judge Symmes. Eloping while the judge was away on business, the couple were married November 25, 1795.

Anna and William Harrison had ten children, a boisterous brood whose education was a constant source of concern to their mother. Tutors were seldom easily found in the Territory, but Anna hired them whenever possible, encouraging other children of the settlement to come to her home whenever "school" was in session. When no tutors were available she taught them herself, careful not to omit a thorough religious education. An omnivorous reader, Anna had become a student of the history of religion, emerging deeply committed to the Presbyterian faith.

Anna's dream of peaceful retirement years with William turned into a nightmare of Whig "log cabin and hard cider" campaigning. She blamed not only his sycophantic friends but drafty, unhealthy conditions in the White House for his illness and death. Living on in the wilderness she loved, Anna stayed with her son John supervising the early education of his little boy, Benjamin, who would become twenty-second President of the United States. Survived by only two of her ten children, she died in 1864 at eighty-nine, an indomitable matriarch of the old frontier.

# 10
## Letitia Tyler

THE SMITHSONIAN INSTITUTION .

### White House Invalid

Letitia Tyler, retiring for the night on April 4, 1841, had no idea she would waken before dawn to news that her husband was President of the United States. Two harried riders from the Capital pounding on her door at 5:00 a.m. told of President Harrison's death and delivered the cabinet's message asking Vice-President Tyler to come to Washington immediately.

John Tyler, the "Tyler Too" afterthought of the Whig's smashing 1840 campaign, had already appointed a substitute to function for him as head of the Senate and had returned to his Williamsburg, Virginia, home. The former senator and two-term governor of Virginia had hoped to carry out his new duties as vice-president from there, where his critically-ill wife was most comfortable. However, Harrison's death had deprived the country of a president and the White House of a tenant. Moving rapidly to fill both vacancies, Tyler had himself sworn in as president, despite arguments against its constitutionality, and brought his family to the White House without delay.

The move presented physical difficulties for Letitia, but she understood its necessity. Then fifty years old, partially paralyzed from a stroke, she had been confined to a wheelchair for nearly three years. An active role as First Lady was out of the question. Sixteen years before Louisa Adams had been the last wife of a president to serve as First Lady, and Letitia privately regretted her own inability to share her husband's social life.

Letitia Christian, the Virginia belle John Tyler had wooed for five years with love letters and poetry before her parents consented to their marriage, had been his gentle confidant and homemaker since their wedding in March 1813. Raised on the substantial estate of her parents, Letitia knew the intricacies of managing a large household and took on this responsibility for John, freeing him to pursue the political career he craved. Their large slaveholdings made her job less difficult than it might have been, but Letitia handled all financial matters herself and gave particular attention to the gardens she loved. Her seven children adored their pretty, sweet-tempered mother and, when illness struck, devoted themselves to caring for her without complaint.

At the White House Letitia lived in seclusion. Elderly Dolley Madison, a frequent visitor, helped the Tylers make decisions of social policy and attended the wedding of Letitia's daughter Elizabeth in January 1842. The occasion was Letitia's only public appearance in the White House. Described by her daughter-in-law Priscilla as the loveliest woman there, "far more attractive . . . in her appearance and bearing than any other lady in the room," Letitia received, "in her sweet, gentle, self-possessed way, all the important people who were led up and presented to her."

She died in September 1842, the first wife of a president to die during her husband's term of office. Her death left her family in the White House facing "the loneliness of this large and gloomy mansion—hung with black—its walls echoing our sighs." Loyal to the memory of their mother, Letitia's children took comfort in their father's praise of her. He had told them "I could not hold up for you a better pattern for your imitation than . . . presented to you by your dear mother. You never saw her course marked with precipitation, but on the contrary. . . brought before the tribunal of her judgement . . . all her actions are founded in prudence."

# 11
## Julia Tyler

### First President's Bride

In a secret wedding ceremony June 26, 1844, Julia Gardiner became the bride of President John Tyler and America's new First Lady. The White House, draped in mourning just a few months previously for several dignitaries killed in an explosion on board the steam frigate *Princeton,* had seemed an unlikely place for romance. But President Tyler, a widower whose wife, Letitia, had died over a year before, was a sensitive target, particularly since the *Princeton* tragedy had presented him with a young and beautiful woman in need of comfort.

She was Julia Gardiner, the "Rose of Long Island" whose good looks and hourglass figure had inspired a memorable magazine advertisement when she was only nineteen. A heartbreaker and the subject of many love poems, Julia left hopeful suitors trailing in her fashionable wake from Europe to Washington. Visiting in the Capital, she was an immediate social success, and was among those invited to a cruise on the Potomac aboard the *Princeton* on February 28, 1844.

Julia's pleasant chat belowdecks with Dolley Madison, President Tyler and others was suddenly interrupted by a muffled explosion overhead. The *Princeton's* large experimental gun had blown up, killing the Secretary of the Navy, the Secretary of State, and others, among them wealthy New Yorker David Gardiner, Julia's father. Tyler, turning with Southern gallantry to Miss Gardiner as she collapsed in horror, knew his was more than a compassionate gesture. He had flirted with Julia and she with him at lighthearted gatherings, and it was even rumored that he had proposed to her, receiving an immediate, "No, no, no!"

The President, of course, was fifty-four and Julia thirty years younger. Their May-December relationship stood open to teasing and ridicule until the funeral at the White House brought them together in circumstances beyond frivolity. With her father gone, Tyler's age seemed an asset, and his wealth and position a secure haven to Julia. Before long, her admiration had turned to ardor and she agreed to marry him. After the wedding in New York the newlyweds faced more critics than well-wishers, for not all Tyler's children accepted their youthful stepmother. Nor was Washington society pleased at being denied the first marriage of a President during his term of office.

For the first time in many years, a socially active First Lady ruled in Washington. Following her wedding reception in the Blue Room, Julia wrote home, "I have commenced my auspicious reign and am in quiet possession of the Presidential Mansion." It did not remain quiet for long. The flurry Julia had caused abroad at the French court in her debut days paled beside her sensational White House entertaining. Surrounded by a

THE BETTMANN ARCHIVE, INC.

Left: Explosion of experimental gun aboard the frigate *Princeton*. Among the eight persons killed was Julia Gardiner's father.

Right: This department store advertisement brought Julia Gardiner instant notoriety and sonnets to "the Rose of Long Island."

dozen maids of honor, a diadem winking in her hair, "Her Serene Loveliness" held court, shrewdly timing her parties according to the political climate and introducing a lively new dance, the polka, to Washington society.

Fiercely loyal to John, she was more upset with his critics than with her own. She hated the nickname "Veto President," and wept when he was burned in effigy. His successful annexation of Texas was her own greatest triumph. Shunning other jewelry, she wore the gold pen with which he had signed the Annexation Bill as a pendant at James Polk's Inauguration.

Still newlyweds when they left the White House, Julia and John moved to Sherwood Forest, his Virginia estate, where they raised a second family of seven children. Most of Tyler's children by his first wife, Letitia, liked Julia, but indications were she had not won all of them over entirely. Julia had broken with her own family during the Civil War, for her sympathies were decidedly Southern despite her New York upbringing.

John's death in 1862 did not alter her loyalties. The Confederacy gave him a hero's funeral; the federal government ignored the passing of its tenth President. Until her own death in 1889, Julia suffered indignities and economic hardship. During the war, her estate had been plundered and the Tyler papers burned. A convert to Catholicism in later years, she returned to Washington where she supervised the education of her two youngest children.

A staunch defender of her husband's political record, Julia had supported John's plans to serve in the Confederate Congress. In 1862, while he was in Richmond attending a session, Julia dreamt of his death. Rushing to Richmond, she was relieved to find him well, but his sudden death shortly afterward, fulfilling her dream, haunted Julia for the rest of her life.

MUSEUM OF THE CITY OF NEW YORK

# 12
## Sarah Polk

### Secretary to the President

Sarah Polk, a commemorative fan wilting in her damp grasp, gazed at the umbrella-swollen throng gathered for her husband's Inauguration. Unprotected from the downpour herself the new First Lady stood unflinching, her sodden black ringlets framing a proud face. She and James had worked virtually day and night the past few months, preparing a "great program" of expansion amid echoes of the Democratic winning campaign slogan of "54° 40′ or Fight!"

But Sarah realized that their own efforts would have been meaningless without the support of Andrew Jackson. "Daughter," her "Uncle Andrew" had said, "I will see you in the White House if it costs me my life," and he had made good his promise, engineering the nomination of dark-horse Polk when the Democrats seemed hopelessly deadlocked between General Lewis Cass and Martin Van Buren. Like her husband, Jackson had favored expansion and exerted his enormous influence on Polk's behalf when Van Buren refused to declare for Texas.

The President and First Lady took their new positions very seriously. James had declared his intention to serve only one term, thus ensuring that his policies would remain unaffected by electioneering purposes. Their one concession to frivolity was a brief appearance at the Inaugural Ball, during which all dancing was halted in deference to them, for they did not dance. In a rich blue velvet gown, her cape heavy with fringe, Sarah greeted each guest, then departed with James. Believing that an elected official had been "hired to work," the President was reluctant to waste time in idle socializing.

James' responsibilities would be Sarah's too, because for the first time a First Lady would take on a political role as well as a social one. Mrs. Polk, for two decades her husband's tireless, trusted assistant, would serve officially as his confidential secretary,

PAINTING BY G. P. A. HEALY, JAMES KNOX POLK MEMORIAL AUXILIARY

a post for which she was well-qualified. Sent as a youngster from her home town of Murfreesboro, Tennessee, to Salem Female Academy, in Salem, North Carolina, she had been educated by the Moravians, emerging as an intellectual and thoroughly disciplined young lady. Politically she was unusually astute for a woman, for her thinking had been molded in her early years by Andrew Jackson and, later, refined by her husband as she took an active part in his political career.

It had been said that Jackson had promoted the Polks' romance as well as their career, a charge that did neither a disservice. His approval, however, may have been all the courting couple needed to cement their relationship, for they shared more than his friendship. Both were serious, industrious, and exceedingly moral. They neither played cards, drank, nor danced, thriving instead on lively conversation about politics. At Sarah's prodding, James ran successfully for the state

Commemorative fan carried by Mrs. Polk
at her husband's Inauguration.

JAMES KNOX POLK MEMORIAL AUXILIARY

legislature in 1823, postponing their wedding until after the election. They were married January 1, 1824, and together began a twenty-year climb to the White House.

Sarah, born in 1803, the well-bred daughter of Joel Childress, was more than a social asset to her aspiring husband. Soon after their marriage she undertook to ease his work load by scanning newspapers for him and filing reports on his constituency. In 1825 James left the state legislature for Congress. There he served with distinction as Speaker of the House between 1835 and 1839. Having no children, Sarah had continued to involve herself in his career, helping with paper work and taking the place of several subordinates. Elected governor of Tennessee in 1839, Polk returned home. His career, far from being over when he lost two reelection bids for governor, reached its apex when he defeated Clay for the presidency in 1844.

Having achieved their success without compromising their stern moral code, the Polks did not change their habits after moving into the White House. Sarah permitted neither dancing nor card playing and served no wine or other alcoholic beverages, even at state dinners.

Unlike early presidents who had vast landholdings and private fortunes, the Polks' means were modest. Sarah had no intention of dipping into their retirement savings to fund lavish receptions. Budgeting her husband's annual salary carefully, she declined to offer refreshments of any kind at her twice-weekly receptions. Opening the White House to the public at these times was, perhaps, more important than the absence of food. Complimented on the decorum shown at one of her parties, Mrs. Polk replied, "Sir, I have never seen it otherwise."

Such piety and austerity in the White House was not wholly inappropriate, for the nation was, after all, at war with Mexico.

Soldiers back from the front were encouraged to bring news of the campaign to the Executive Mansion, where Sarah, if a party were in progress, silenced her guests while the officer reported to the President.

It was difficult indeed to find fault with a First Lady whose only weakness appeared to be the strength of her convictions. Refusing all favors, Sarah would not even accept bouquets from the federal conservatory. Well-known, too, was the fact that she worked fourteen or more hours a day with James, keeping his counsel and assisting in countless ways. Although her witty conversation was much admired, she took care not to accept credit for political decisions, always prefacing her comments with "Mr. Polk says."

James' rapidly declining health troubled Sarah deeply in the months before Zachary Taylor took over the presidency. Retirement to Polk Place, their Nashville home, would restore him, she thought. But Polk's crushing work load, borne with only three days' vacation in the past four years, had totally drained his physical reserves. He died in June 1849, just a few months after leaving office, whispering on his deathbed, "I love you, Sarah, for all eternity, I love you."

Mrs. Polk's assertion that she and Polk Place "Belonged to the Nation" was no idle claim. She opened her home to the public, never leaving it herself except to attend church, until her own death in 1891. During the Civil War, despite the location of her home, and her own probable Southern sympathies, the Union Army took pains to protect her and her mementos. They even brought some of their own valuables to her for safekeeping. The discretion which had been so much a part of her political life continued, for she kept her opinions to herself. Long after the slavery issue was resolved, when questioned, she said simply, "The War settled all that."

# 13
## Margaret Taylor

### A Better Soldier*

Ill and wretchedly unhappy when her husband was elected president in 1848, Margaret did not travel with "Old Rough and Ready" to Washington. Zachary's unwelcome triumph was even more devastating to her than his nomination, which she had reportedly denounced as "a plot to deprive her of his society and shorten his life." In her small cottage in Baton Rouge, Louisiana, where she had prayed every night for Zachary's defeat, Margaret steeled herself for the journey to Washington.

The move was more difficult than any Margaret had faced before, although, a devoted army wife, she had followed Zachary to lonely outposts from Michigan to Florida. Now, a semi-invalid in her sixties, she followed him once again, this time to the White House. Sick and weary, she lived in seclusion, unconcerned that Capital gossips speculated that the new First Lady was not ailing at all but would not appear socially because she was an uncouth pipe smoker and "poor white of the wilds." These charges were patently false, for Margaret, who hated the smell of tobacco, was Maryland gentry; daughter of plantation heir Walter Smith, and granddaughter of General James Mackall.

Lieutenant Zachary Taylor, on leave at his Kentucky homestead in 1809, saw Margaret Smith while she visited her sister nearby. They were married in June 1810, leaving for the Indiana Territory the following year. Serving under William Henry Harrison, Zachary fought the Indians and defended Fort Knox against Tecumseh. Margaret shared garrison life with her husband, and struggled to raise a family of four daughters in the shadow of Indian raids and rampant disaster. In 1819, a welcome transfer from desolate Green Bay, Wisconsin, to Louisiana brought grief when their two youngest daughters died of malaria in the Bayou country. This loss left permanent scars, even after another girl

and a son were born. Thereafter, the Taylors refused to expose their children to similar danger, sending them to relatives for safekeeping and education. But sorrow continued to stalk them. In 1835 their daughter Knox died of malaria just three months after her wedding to Jefferson Davis.

Needing her strong-willed husband more than ever, Margaret tramped doggedly with him from post to post as he continued to distinguish himself in the Black Hawk and Seminole wars. At last, in 1841, considering future campaigns and separations unlikely, they settled down on the Misssissippi, only to have the Mexican War thrust Zachary into prominence as Santa Anna's conqueror.

Finding the presidency a cruel reward for her husband's heroism at Buena Vista, Margaret remained hidden in her White House suite. She was far removed from inner debates on stopping the spread of slavery and holding the nation together. She enjoyed listening to the Marine Band when it played on the south lawn, but was not well enough to stroll outside with Zachary during the concerts. Saving her energy for small family dinners, "The invalid, full of interest in the passing show in which she had not the strength to take part, talked most agreeably and kindly. . .and ably bore her share of conversation at the table."

Just sixteen months after Zachary became President, his wife's fears that it would shorten his life were realized. He died suddenly July 9, 1850, after long exposure to the summer sun during cornerstone-laying ceremonies at the Washington Monument. The nation was stunned; Margaret nearly destroyed. During the state funeral she "lay without uttering a sound, but trembled silently from head to foot as one band after another blared the funeral music."

Worn to a shadow, she died in 1852, mourned by those who recalled her husband's praise, "She was a better soldier than I was."

*No known portrait exists.*

# 14
## Abigail Fillmore

THE SMITHSONIAN INSTITUTION

### First Lady of the Library

The solemn moment when her husband was sworn in as President of the United States was lost to Abigail Fillmore. In poor health when Millard was elected vice-president, she had spent little time in Washington, preferring to remain at home in Buffalo, New York. There she learned of Zachary Taylor's death and her husband's succession to the presidency July 10, 1850.

Joining Millard as soon as possible in the "temple of inconveniences" as he called the White House, Abigail faced the same "unhealthy conditions" reputed to have contributed to the untimely deaths of Harrison, Polk and Taylor. Correcting some of these "conditions," she had water pipes and a bathtub installed, and replaced the huge kitchen fireplace with a monumental iron range.

There were no books in the mansion, not even a Bible, a situation the new First Lady, a former schoolteacher, likely considered more critical than the absence of modern plumbing. Abigail moved swiftly to obtain an appropriation from Congress to establish a White House library, a project which Millard enthusiastically endorsed. They enjoyed evenings together in the upstairs Oval Room where, in addition to the library, Abigail had installed her harp and her piano.

Books had always meant a great deal to Abigail. They were virtually the only legacy her father, Lemuel Powers, a Baptist minister, had left to his family. His library had helped Abigail augment her own education so that, at sixteen, she was able to teach summers and earn enough to attend an academy in winter. In 1819, when she was twenty-one, Millard Fillmore, an only slightly younger student, joined her class in New Hope, New York, determined to obtain an education. Before long Abigail's instruction spilled out of the classroom, flooding their lives. Their schoolbook romance lasted eight years, during which Millard began studying law.

After their marriage in February 1826, Abigail continued to teach, a daring departure from custom for a new bride. With immense pride in her husband's achievements, she watched him rise in the Whig party from congressman and state comptroller to vice-president. She had thought his career had reached its zenith, unable to foresee Taylor's death, which catapulted Fillmore into the White House in a time of extreme political sectionalism.

Millard Fillmore appreciated the effort his wife made to entertain as First Lady, giving Tuesday receptions and Friday levees, for he knew she was not strong and an old leg injury made prolonged standing painful. Their stay in the White House was short, for the Whigs denied Fillmore their nomination in 1852, chiefly because he had signed the Fugitive Slave Act. In the few remaining months of his administration, Fillmore took greater pleasure than ever in joining his wife, son and daughter during the evenings in Abigail's library, the upstairs oval room where she had arranged her books, her harp and her piano.

Franklin Pierce's election brought Fillmore's administration to an end in an unusually courteous, nearly friendly transfer of powers. Determined to attend the Inauguration as a gesture of respect, Abigail was undeterred by snow and bone-chilling winds. Developing pneumonia, she died just a few weeks after leaving the White House.

Lonely without Abigail who had been "eight years my sweetheart, and twenty-seven my wife," Millard married a widow, Caroline Carmichael McIntosh, in 1858.

# 15
## Jane Pierce

NEW HAMPSHIRE HISTORICAL SOCIETY

### "Shadow in the White House"

Franklin Pierce weathered the Inaugural winds alone in March 1853. Bowed with indescribable grief and anguish, his wife, Jane, had forced herself to accompany him as far as Baltimore but could go no further. Their eleven-year-old son, Benny, had died before their eyes in a train wreck less than two months before and Jane's already fragile spirit had snapped.

It was not her first sorrow, for Benny had been their sole surviving child. He had had two younger brothers, both of whom were dead. Then, too, Jane suffered from tuberculosis and was additionally burdened with Franklin's alcoholism, conditions which their personal bereavement did nothing to improve. Even when she had recovered sufficiently to come to the White House, Mrs. Pierce was unable to assert herself as First Lady.

When they were married in November 1834, it had seemed that young Congressman Pierce had chosen a bride who would add to his political stature. Indeed, his "dearest Jeanie," whose father, Reverend Jesse Appleton, had been president of Bowdoin College, came from an impeccable New England family. But Washington held no allure for Jane Pierce. Its climate weakened her, its society depressed her, and its notoriety frightened her. She had spent one session of Congress there, and later returned when her husband was elected to the Senate. She continued to long for New Hampshire and begged Franklin to abandon politics for a legal practice in New England.

Eventually he did so, even turning down an appointment as Polk's attorney general because of "Mrs. Pierce's health." The outbreak of the war with Mexico in 1846, however, presented a challenge to Pierce unlike any he had encountered in the political arena. Deaf to Jane's entreaties that he remain at home, he enlisted as a private and soon became a colonel of volunteers. A year later he was a brigadier-general under Winfield Scott in the advance on Mexico City. In 1852, against his wife's wishes, Franklin allowed his name to be placed in nomination by the Democrats and won as a compromise candidate on the forty-ninth ballot. The messenger who brought word of Pierce's nomination saw Jane faint when he gave her the news. Her son, Benny, as distressed as she, told his mother, "I hope he won't be elected, for I should not like to be at Washington and I know you would not either."

Had Benny lived, Jane might have found life in the Capital endurable, if not pleasant; without him it was agonizing. After two years, Jane finally attempted a public appearance, but "her woe-begone face, with its sunken dark eyes and skin like yellowed ivory, banished all animation in others." Even the waxy, wired camellia bouquets she placed in the White House embodied her melancholy.

Nor was the national mood uplifting. Enraged by *Uncle Tom's Cabin*, slavery and anti-slavery factions polarized further. Pro-Southern Pierce, signing the Kansas-Nebraska Bill, unleashed "Bloody Kansas," ending his political career with the finality his wife's efforts had never achieved.

Buchanan's election in 1856 freed the Pierces to return to New Hampshire, where Franklin hoped Jane would regain her strength. But when the "Northern man with Southern principles" left the White House, his wife was so racked with grief and consumption she had to be carried. She died December 2, 1863.

# 16
## Mary Lincoln

### Clouded by Controversy

"He is to be President of the United States some day; if I had not thought so, I would not have married him, for you can see he is not pretty. But look at him! Doesn't he look as if he would make a magnificent President?" Mary Lincoln, her plump cheeks pink with pride, saw that her husband did indeed make a "magnificent President." It was March 4, 1861, and her prediction, made long ago when Abraham had first been elected to Congress, had come true. The half-finished dome of the Capitol, an unwitting symbol of the imperfection of the Union, loomed behind Lincoln as he took the oath of office. With the tinderbox of secession exploding in his face, Lincoln stepped up to greatness, draining his every reserve of intellect, fortitude and courage. His wife, who might have lightened his burden, made it heavier still, for Mary, subject to "spells" of yet-undiagnosed mental illness, required tender handling.

She hardly seemed the same woman Lincoln had wed in 1842 with a gold band inscribed, "Love is eternal." Mary Todd was a witty, self-possessed belle socially superior to her backwoods husband. A member of the prominent Todd family of Lexington, Kentucky, she had been educated at an Episcopal academy and a fine boarding school. Her sister had married the son of the governor of Illinois, and Mary, seeking a similar match, joined her in Springfield. A dimpled dumpling of a girl, Mary was pretty and popular. She had a wry sense of humor and a keen interest in politics, traits that appealed not only to Lincoln, but to another beau, Stephen A. Douglas. Her niece recalled that when Mary met Lincoln at a cotillion he said, "Miss Todd, I want to dance with you in the worst way," inviting her comment, "He certainly did."

Their marriage, after a stormy courtship and once-canceled wedding ceremony, was a social step down for Mary. Abraham, a strug-gling lawyer who liked to tease that "One 'd' was enough for God but not for the Todd's," could offer at first only a room at the Globe Tavern for a home. But Abraham's rise as an attorney and his political success, precarious as it was, thrilled Mary. With high hopes she went to Washington with him when he was elected to Congress in 1847, but was disappointed in her failure to make any social impact on the Capital and soon left.

Lincoln's brief term in the House over, years of political frustration followed amidst the death throes of the Whig party. Then, joining the Republicans, he ran against Stephen Douglas for the Senate in 1858. He lost the election but won a national reputation debating with his opponent. Two years later he was nominated for the presidency. Hearing the news, his first thoughts were for his wife. "There's a little woman down our house would like to hear this," he said. "I'll go down and tell her." Months later, told he had received the majority of electoral votes, Lincoln again rushed home to Mary, waking her to say, "We are elected!"

But the reality of his election lacked the glory of the dream they had shared, for, as the presidential train chugged closer to the Capital, cheering Northern crowds became jeering Southern ones. Finally rumors of an assassination plot forced Lincoln to abandon the train and slip secretly into Washington. Left to face the sullen Capital alone, the new First Lady's arrival was less than auspicious. The matron who came to the White House from the midwest on the fashionable heels of Harriet Lane, bachelor President Buchanan's exquisite niece and hostess, knew she would suffer by comparison. Mary's social credentials were impeccable in Illinois, but she was ill-prepared to meet Parisian-gowned Southern belles on their home ground. They had manipulated Washington society for some time, and had no intention of bowing to an eccentric little woman from Springfield.

Confronted with such sophisticated competition, Mrs. Lincoln counterattacked by ordering a new wardrobe, telling Elizabeth Keckly, her "modiste," "I must dress in costly materials. The people scrutinize every article that I wear with critical curiosity. The very fact of having grown up in the West subjects me to more searching observation." Her shopping soon became an obsession as she struggled pathetically to out-dress and out-maneuver the brittle women who mocked her.

The blinding headaches which had stabbed deep into her brain from the time she was very young came on more frequently in Washington. Her "nervous spells," as Lincoln called them, attacked without warning, causing violent rages, prolonged weeping, or lightning mood changes. Patient, unfailingly kind, Lincoln kept close watch over his wife. When friends noticed him staring at her during a party, he betrayed no concern, chuckling, "My wife is as handsome as when she was a girl, and I, a poor nobody then, fell in love with her; and what is more, I have never fallen out."

But soothing Mary was the least of Lincoln's problems. Fort Sumter had been fired upon by Confederate troops April 12, 1861, plunging the country into war. Washington, really a Southern city despite its function as the national capital, seethed with hatred. Mary Todd was despised by Southern sympathizers as a vulgar turncoat to her Kentucky heritage. Northerners accused her of being a Confederate spy. With many of her family fighting for the South, Mary's loyalty to the Union was constantly questioned. Threatening letters piled up until she asked her secretary to screen her mail before she saw it. Her secretary, William Stoddard, understood her motives went deeper than just sparing herself the task of reading such "hate mail." He said, "You know why she wishes you to

inspect her letters. The President's wife is venomously accused of being at heart a traitor, and of being in communication with the Confederate authorities."

Even this precaution failed to stop the "stabs given Mary." The Committee on the Conduct of the War called a hearing to investigate her loyalty. Only Lincoln's testimony, "I, of my own knowledge, know that it is untrue that any of my family hold treasonable communication with the enemy," brought a halt to their proceedings.

Lincoln protected her against such false charges, but did not curtail the shopping sprees that gave her so much pleasure. The only time she seemed truly happy was when she fluttered over silks and laces, selecting new finery. He indulged her weakness, even though he realized extravagance was not appropriate at a time of national deprivation. He did not know, however, the extent of her purchases. She had charged great sums, her debt pyramiding, until she feared his failure to win reelection would ruin them. "I do not know what would become of us all. . .there is more at stake in this election than he dreams of. I have contracted large debts of which he knows nothing, and which he will be unable to pay if he is defeated."

Unable to control her spending, Mary tried to compensate by extreme frugality in the running of her household. She dismissed the White House steward and much of the staff, setting off sharp volleys of criticism. A columnist complained, "State dinners could have been dispensed with, without a word of blame, had their cost been consecrated to the soldiers' service, but when it was made apparent that they were omitted from personal penuriousness and a desire to devote their cost to personal gratification, the public censure knew no bounds." Mary's other money-saving schemes met with equal hostility because her personal extravagance continued.

"Prodigal in personal expenditure, she brought shame on the President's House by petty economies which had never disgraced it before. Had the milk of its dairy been sent to the hospitals, she would have received golden praise. But the whole city felt scandalized to have it haggled over and peddled from the back door of the White House."

Mary, already teetering on a slim mental tightrope, was plunged into a clinging web of despair by her son Willie's death in 1862. Twelve years before she had lost Edward, her second son, and in the interim had endured the deformities of Robert, her eldest, and little Tad. Robert's crossed eyes had been fixed with a risky operation, but Tad, born with a cleft palate, would always speak with difficulty. It might have been easy, under these conditions, to understand Mary's morbid fears for her children's health, but the war had tipped the nation's perspective. Sons were sent off to die in "Mr. Lincoln's War," and at least one bitter mother thought Mary fortunate to have seen her son die, rather than having to send him out to be shot.

Few of her good deeds received any publicity at all, for Mary ignored the advice of her secretary who urged her to "sweeten the contents of many journals" by taking reporters along when she went to visit sick soldiers. Penny-pinching in many ways, she was sometimes as generous with others as she was lavish with her wardrobe, for she contributed often to help starving Negroes who had their freedom, but no food.

Still, she shopped. She raged at her husband, shrieked at her staff, and finally, misbehaved in public. Confined to her own home, her peculiarities merely generated gossip but, aired in public, they became a scandal. She had carried on outrageously at a field inspection while riding with Mrs. Grant, when she spotted Abraham cantering alongside the attractive wife of General Ord. The young

LIBRARY OF CONGRESS

41

DISTRICT OF COLUMBIA PUBLIC LIBRARY

Black-draped catafalque for Lincoln's body in the East Room. Mary Lincoln was unable to accompany the funeral cortege.

woman had burst into tears, while Mrs. Grant tried to calm Mary, who spat, "I suppose you think you'll get to the White House yourself, don't you?"

Lincoln was eventually forced to admit to himself that Mary's behavior was abnormal. Since Willie's death her headaches had grown worse, and a severe head injury she had sustained in July 1863 added to her misery. She had been thrown from the seat of her carriage after it had been tampered with in an apparent attempt to kill the President. Two years later her son Robert said, "I think Mother has never quite recovered from the effects of her fall." Lincoln sadly agreed. "The caprices of Mrs. Lincoln, I am satisfied, are the result of partial insanity," he said. Those who feared that Mrs. Lincoln could unduly influence her husband would have been relieved by his admission, for Mary often commented that her husband was "no judge of men" and that he relied on her knowledge of human nature.

But the triumph of her husband's reelection temporarily cheered Mary. She attended the second Inaugural Ball, buoyed by an expensive gown and accessories. The following month, thrilled with Lee's surrender at Appomattox, she and Abraham planned a Good Friday celebration at Ford's Theatre to see *Our American Cousin*. Sitting close together in their flag-draped box, Mary and Abraham held hands during the third act. Suddenly Lincoln's hand went limp. The assassin had struck.

Lincoln's nightmare about a funeral in the East Room with a soldier saying, "The President was killed by an assassin," had come true. Mary Lincoln, totally unhinged, lay weeping in the White House for five weeks, while her husband's funeral cortege went on to Springfield without her. As Lincoln's widow Mary was even more passionately reviled than she had been as his wife. He was the martyred President, and the unhappiness he had suffered on her account made her a hated villain.

Fears of poverty consumed her, though she was not really in want. She tried to raise money by selling her clothes, and this created a scandal. Claiming the Republicans owed her a patronage debt and should contribute to her support, she alienated the handful of people who might have defended her. Tales that she had stripped the White House of its furnishings when she left were revived. Souvenir hunters had actually been responsible for the pillaging while Mary lay prostrate in a guest chamber for over a month.

Living abroad to escape her enemies, she traveled for six weary years with Tad. Completely dependent on her son, she had said, "Only my darling Tad keeps me from taking my life." His sudden death after their return to the United States probably destroyed any vestige of sanity she had left, for her behavior thereafter became so irrational Robert Lincoln moved to have her committed. She was declared insane and placed in an institution in May 1875. Several months later, however, she was released "restored to health." Blind, she thought from weeping, and paralyzed, she died July 16, 1882.

A creature more scorned than pitied during her lifetime, Mary Todd's character was considered in a different light only after her death when an autopsy revealed that she had suffered from a "cerebral disease." But these findings, conclusive though they seemed, did not end the speculation about this tortured woman. The nature of the disease, its extent and the length of time it had tormented her remain a mystery. Contemporary chroniclers showed her little mercy; early biographers tried to ignore her faults; recent historians accepted mental illness as an excuse for all her actions. The truth, perhaps, lies somewhere in between.

# 17
## Eliza Johnson

LIBRARY OF CONGRESS

### Her Husband's Teacher

Eliza Johnson, sleeping in the gray morning hours of April 15, 1865, did not know Abraham Lincoln had been assassinated. Her peaceful Tennessee home was far from Washington, where her husband, grim with shock, had been sworn in as president. The news, when it reached her, was every bit as devastating as Andrew feared. "Almost deranged" with worry that Andrew, too, would be murdered, his invalid wife prepared to join him in the Capital. Wasted from tuberculosis, she was not really fit for travel and could not act officially as First Lady.

Since the couple's marriage in 1827, when Eliza was sixteen and Andrew eighteen, they had overcome many hardships together. Andrew, never having been to school, was barely literate; Eliza, despite her youth, was a teacher. In their crowded little room behind Andrew's tailor shop in Greeneville, Tennessee, she taught her husband how to read and write. They struggled against poverty, too, for Eliza had known little else in her mountain town. Her father, John McCardle, a Scotch-Irish shoemaker, had died when she was small, and her mother had made quilts and sandals to support herself.

But Eliza was a good teacher and a frugal housewife. She managed Andrew's earnings well as he practiced the tailor's trade he had learned in North Carolina before crossing the Great Smokies to Greeneville. According to local gossip, he had sought out Eliza because she had been the only girl who had not laughed at his travel-weary appearance when he arrived in town. If people had laughed at him they did not do so for long. His success in local politics led to election to the state legislature, Congress, and eventually the vice-presidency.

Eliza supported his politics completely, knowing him to be an exceptional man. She backed him even when, as a border state senator during the Civil War, his anti-secession views meant real danger to her and their four children. The rebels seized Greeneville, turning "traitor Johnson's" home into a barracks and his wife into the street. Continuing to help guerrilla fighters, Eliza slipped food to their hideouts. At the mercy of the rebels, she wandered from town to town, her health broken, until at last, crossing enemy lines, she was reunited with Andrew.

She had suffered much at the hands of the Confederates, but Eliza approved Andrew's compassionate Reconstruction policies. Republican radicals did not. Their ire culminated with impeachment proceedings when President Johnson dismissed Secretary of War Stanton. At this time of trial, the First Family's dignity was remarkable. From her tiny "upper room" Eliza generated courage and optimism, insisting the White House routine remain undisturbed. Her daughter, Martha Patterson, carried on as First Lady with admirable calm. Before Andrew's death in 1875, and her own in 1876, Eliza saw her husband thoroughly vindicated by election to the Senate, and her own fortitude in the face of his impeachment was not overlooked. Colonel Crook, who brought her the news of Andrew's acquittal, remembered:

> Tears were in her eyes, but her voice was firm and she did not tremble once as she said "I knew he'd be acquitted; I knew it.". . .I shall never forget the picture of that feeble, wasted little woman standing so proudly and assuring me so positively that she had never doubted for one instant that her beloved husband would be proved innocent. . .

43

# 18
## Julia Grant

### "Garden Spot of Orchids"

Oblivious to the unfortunate chaos of the Inaugural Ball held in the Treasury Building, Julia Grant embarked on her "beautiful dream." She seemed unaware that construction dust in the new wing was choking many of her guests, and that few of them in the crush had been served supper. She knew only that her husband, so many times a failure, was the President of the United States, swept into the White House with the slogan, "Let us have peace."

The Executive Mansion, long dormant as the Capital's social hub, revived quickly with Julia Grant as its mistress. Lavishly, lovingly, she decorated it in Victorian splendor, and transformed dull state dinners into twenty-nine-course Continental feasts. The new First Lady had some thought of transforming herself as well, for her warm brown eyes were crossed, and a recently developed operation to correct them tempted her. But "Ulyss" had other ideas. Telling her he liked her the way that she was, he dismissed the idea of surgery.

Grant may have been the only man who thought Julia beautiful, but he was the only one who counted. She was the sister of one of his West Point classmates, and he readily admitted having fallen in love with her at first sight, bucking her father's opposition to their marriage for four years. Colonel Dent's objections were understandable. A wealthy slaveholder, he had raised his daughter at White Haven, a thousand-acre estate near St. Louis. Julia had loved private school, where she studied "history, mythology and the things I happened to like." She loved music, too, taking instrumental and voice lessons. Marriage to an army man, her father felt, would be wholly unsatisfactory for his classics-oriented daughter. Further, he could not imagine her giving up her domestic servants to live on a military pittance at a distant army post. Eventually, with re-

COURTESY CHICAGO HISTORICAL SOCIETY

luctance, he gave his consent, but war with Mexico separated the couple before they could be married. In August 1848, back from service under Zachary Taylor, Grant claimed his bride at last.

Julia adapted quickly to life as an army wife, spending her first winter at a bleak, forsaken post on Lake Ontario. Transferred to Detroit, she returned home briefly for the birth of her first son and visited Ulysses' parents in 1852 when the second of her three boys was born. Then Grant was ordered to the Pacific coast, a rigorous trip that precluded taking his family. Without Julia things did not go well for him. Previously she had encouraged him to give up drinking, and he had, even joining a temperance lodge and heading its marches. Without her, in the West, he lost his resolve. When his commander reprimanded him for his drinking, he resigned his commission.

Turning to another career, farming, he and Julia struggled to make "Hardscrabble," their land outside St. Louis, pay. But four barren years later, during which Grant had even cut and sold firewood to make ends

LIBRARY OF CONGRESS

East Room of the White House after redecoration by President and Mrs. Grant in 1873.

meet, they were forced to auction off their farm. Thereafter one job disappointment led to another until, in desperation, Grant and Julia returned to Galena, Illinois, where he helped his father in the tanning business. Then he joined the Union Army, and the Civil War, which had gobbled up a tanner's clerk, spat out a general.

Mary Lincoln detested him, labeling Grant a "butcher," but Abraham said, "I can't spare him—he's a fighter." So was his wife. Knowing how much her presence meant to him, Julia followed whenever possible, often bringing the children. In Mississippi, when the Holly Springs garrison was captured, she slipped through enemy lines, barely escaping with her four-year-old son, Jesse. Her oldest son, Fred, just thirteen, even rode with his father to the ragged edges of combat. Then victory at Appomattox blossomed into victory at the polls when the Republicans nominated Grant for the presidency.

With advice from army engineers, Ulysses and Julia remodeled the White House. Grecian columns and crystal chandeliers sprouting opaque, swollen globes decorated the East Room. There Julia's receptions were held, and her daughter, Nellie, was married in a White House wedding unequaled in floral and confectionery display. But Julia's extravagance was not criticized as Mary Lincoln's had been. She even summered at fashionable Long Branch, New Jersey, and visited Martha's Vineyard without reproach. It was clear that Julia Grant had disarmed jealous Capital hostesses by asking cabinet wives and other prominent women to assist her at White House functions. At her open houses, however, "chambermaids elbowed countesses and all enjoyed themselves."

It was probably for these reasons that Julia's popularity remained undimmed by the scandals that beset Grant's administration, although it was true that he discussed all his appointments with her. Their son recalled, "No one understood better than father that by each appointment he set a light or dug a pit. . .evening after evening, he talked with mother. . .'The country needs, I must find, a good man — the best possible.'" He rarely succeeded. His private secretary, O.E. Babcock, was charged with participating in the Whiskey Ring, and Secretary of War Belknap resigned when it was revealed that he had received enormous sums in kickbacks from the sale of trading posts in the West. Early in Grant's first administration, his own brother-in-law had been exposed as a participant in the Fiske and Gould "Black Friday" gold manipulations.

Julia was reluctant to leave the White House, even after her husband's second term, for she was happier there than she had ever been in her life. It had been a "feast of cleverness and wit" which she wished "might have continued forever except that it would have deterred others from enjoying the same privilege." Regretfully she and Ulysses left for a two-year trip abroad, where they were fêted as if they were still President and First Lady. Home again, they settled in New York, hoping to build on borrowed assets by starting a brokerage firm, but Ulysses, the perennial business failure, was doomed once more. In three years he was bankrupt.

But the Civil War, which had rescued him before, saved him again. He prepared his memoirs of the war, hoping his royalties would support Julia after his death. He completed the last volume before he died in 1885, succeeding, at the end, in providing for his wife, who survived him by seventeen years.

Julia never tired, as the years passed, of recalling the "bright and beautiful dream" she had shared with her husband in the White House. It was, she said wistfully, "a garden spot of orchids."

# 19
## Lucy Hayes

### "Lemonade Lucy"

Already en route to the Capital for her husband's Inauguration, Lucy Hayes was relieved to hear that Rutherford had at last been officially declared president-elect. She had left Ohio with grave misgivings, for in spite of the impending Inauguration, the 1876 Hayes-Tilden contest was still in doubt. Tilden's popular majority had been nullified by Hayes' electoral college victory, but questions regarding the validity of some electoral votes had sparked a full election review. With remarkable outward calm Lucy had weathered months of concern with Rutherford, refusing to be baited by politicians charging election fraud.

The Inauguration, too, was plagued with irregularities. Grant's term legally expired March 3, at midnight, but March 4, 1877, was a Sunday, and Hayes' Inauguration would therefore take place Monday, March 5. Anticipating the difficulties of an "interim" situation, President Grant arranged a midnight oath-taking for Hayes in the White House. To Lucy Hayes, however, the public ceremony next day was infinitely more meaningful. Her husband's triumph seemed to her a rebirth of honesty and integrity in American politics, replacing the deep discouragement she had felt election night when early returns had indicated a Tilden machine victory.

The new First Lady was, perhaps, unaware that her own appearance was equally reassuring to the uneasy crowd. Dressed in black, lace frothing at her neck, Lucy's "singularly gentle and winning face" impressed observers with its Madonna-like beauty. It was not only her lovely face, however, that had endeared Lucy to Rutherford years before. Compared even to "city belles," he said, "I do not see anyone who makes me forget the natural gaiety and attractiveness of Miss Lucy. . . . By George, I am in love with her!" Hayes wrote in his diary. He proposed to Lucy and they were married December 30, 1852.

The bride's education and antecedents were both extraordinary. Lucy Webb had graduated with highest honors from Wesleyan Women's College, having also attended Ohio Wesleyan University. Her father, Dr. James Webb, and her mother were both descended from prominent participants in the American Revolution, and their Ohio land, in part, was a government gift in recognition of their antecedents' service.

The outbreak of the Civil War found Lucy firmly behind the Union, wishing she were at Fort Sumter "with a garrison of women." Her hatred of slavery had surpassed Rutherford's, but he soon shared her views. In 1856 he rejected the faltering Whigs, joining the Republicans, who had declared their opposition to slavery. Accepting a major's commission, Hayes fought with the Twenty-third Ohio Regiment early in the war. When he was wounded in September 1862, Lucy had her chance to do something in the field. She nursed him back to health, then occupied herself in caring for other wounded for the remainder of the war.

Hayes, a well-known Cincinnati lawyer before the war and now a hero, was elected to Congress before peace was declared. After his term he returned to Ohio as governor, winning reelection twice. Then, a decided underdog in the 1876 presidential election, his minority victory took him to the White House.

While her husband fought for Civil Service reform, the First Lady brought her own influence to bear on other issues. President Grant had left them a gift of wine, which Lucy served at a spring reception. Thereafter, she banned alcoholic beverages from the White House. Inevitably she was dubbed "Lemonade Lucy," a nickname she regarded with some humor. Critics of her ban on liquor found themselves neatly outflanked by an organization of surprising strength. The

46

Women's Christian Temperance Union stood foursquare behind Lucy, praising her extravagantly, and according her their ultimate tribute, "She hath done what she could." Ordering a portrait of her for the White House, they presented Mrs. Hayes with a magnificent sideboard in appreciation of her actions.

Even without liquor, Lucy's receptions were memorable. She prepared bouquets and souvenir charts for her guests, reproducing the menu and names of those present. Rather than renovate the Executive Mansion, she had used much of her appropriation for a unique set of china, depicting nature and wildlife of the United States. Formal entertaining, however, took second place to unpretentious evening gatherings. Lucy received anyone who chose to call after dinner, a move praised as "bright and cheerful and of good report . . . the distinctive social feature of Mrs. Hayes' regime at the White House."

It surprised many that gracious, ladylike Lucy Hayes was something of an outdoorswoman, who regretted that they no longer had time for fishing trips, for Rutherford agreed she was "a matchless fisherwoman." She spent hours digging and weeding the White House gardens, which she felt belonged to the people. When congressmen complained that annual egg-rolling at the Capitol was ruining the grass, she insisted the custom be continued at the White House. Having lost three of her eight children, Lucy loved to be surrounded with lively youngsters.

A devout member of the Methodist Episcopal church, Lucy brought morning prayer services and evening hymn-sings to the Executive Mansion. Rutherford cheerfully took part, admitting, "With no musical taste or cultivation myself, I am yet so fond of simple airs I have often thought I could not love a woman who did not sing them." Love Lucy he did, even renewing their marriage vows in the White House on their twenty-fifth anniversary. He was delighted that his wife wore the same dress in which she had been married.

Because Hayes had declared in advance he would not seek a second term, there was no question of reelection. Pleased with the victory of their friend, James Garfield, Rutherford and Lucy retired to their Spiegel Grove home in Ohio. Until her death in 1889 Lucy Hayes took part in child welfare and missionary work. She was a product of her time, when women's suffrage and other feminist causes were gaining momentum. Because her moral convictions and intellectual achievements were tempered with complete femininity she inspired affection and respect. There was, perhaps, something to the words of the correspondent who said of Lucy Hayes, "I have never seen such a face reign in the White House."

PAINTING BY DANIEL HUNTINGTON, WHITE HOUSE COLLECTION

# 20
## Lucretia Garfield

LAKE COUNTY HISTORICAL SOCIETY, MENTOR, OHIO

### Martyred President's Wife

Learning that her husband had received the Republican nomination for president in 1880 Lucretia Garfield had said, "It is a terrible responsibility to come to him and to me." She did not know how terrible. All omens had pointed to success for James A. Garfield. A stubborn March sun, relenting at the last minute, had burst through leaden skies in time for the Inauguration, and an enthusiastic crowd cheered when James kissed his wife and mother following the ceremony. Even some Confederate veterans had waved an American flag. The new First Lady had every reason to believe her husband's victory had healed the wounds his party had sustained at the convention. There, Stalwarts backing Grant's third-term bid clashed with "reform" forces, until Garfield's dark-horse nomination on the thirty-sixth ballot. In a conciliatory move, Stalwart Chester Alan Arthur was named vice-president.

"Crete," as James called his wife, was content to return to Washington with her five children. It had been her second home for seventeen years while James served in Congress. As First Lady, Lucretia plunged into research, planning to restore the White House on a historically documented basis. Her project was well received, although it left little time for entertaining. She spent most of her day at the Library of Congress, poring over yellowed journals and books. Washington society accepted Mrs. Garfield for what she was—a respected teacher and student of the classics.

Scholarship had always been a way of life to Lucretia. Her father, Zebulon Rudolph, a founder of Western Reserve Eclectic Institute in Hiram, Ohio, insisted his gifted daughter obtain a thorough education. One of her teachers at the Institute was James Garfield, whom she had met before while attending Geauga Seminary. Drawn to one another by a mutual love of the classics, their eight-year "understanding" culminated in marriage on November 11, 1858. Lucretia had embarked on a teaching career, saving scrupulously while James finished his education and established himself as professor, then president, of the college in Hiram. Abhorring slavery, James left his peaceful campus to join the Union Army as a lieutenant colonel, later becoming a general. In 1863 he fought on another front, in Washington, as a newly elected congressman.

His wife was no novice to political infighting. Nearly two decades in the Capital had prepared her well to be the wife of a president. James respected her opinions on important issues, relying strongly on her character assessments. Accepting his appointment as secretary of state, James G. Blaine wrote, "I wish you would say to Mrs. Garfield that the knowledge that she desires me in your Cabinet is more valuable to me than even the desire of the President-elect himself."

An attack of malaria in late spring 1881 drove Mrs. Garfield out of humid Washington to her summer home in Elberon, New Jersey. After his college reunion in July, James planned to join her. As he prepared to leave from the Washington depot on July 2, an assassin shot him twice crying, "I am a Stalwart of the Stalwarts. Arthur is President now." For more than two months Garfield fought death. He even begged to be taken to Elberon, hoping the sea air would revive him. "Frail, fatigued, desperate, but firm," his wife stood by with their five children. He died September 19, 1881. His widow survived him by thirty-six years.

# 21
## Ellen Arthur

LIBRARY OF CONGRESS

### "Ritual of Remembrance"

Accepting the second spot on the Garfield ticket in 1880, Chester Alan Arthur admitted "The office of Vice President is a greater honor than I ever dreamed of attaining." It was an honor he would have given much to share with his wife, Ellen, whose sudden death a few months before had left him in deep mourning. Many joined him in his sorrow for Ellen Arthur had been a popular and much-respected woman. A gifted soprano, she had dedicated her talent to charity and her philanthropies were well known. Mrs. Arthur's death from pneumonia January 12, 1880, had come just three days after she had performed as guest soloist at a benefit concert. Apparently she had caught cold immediately afterward, waiting outside the concert hall for her carriage in the bitter winter night.

Born in Virginia in 1837, Ellen Arthur had come from one of the state's most distinguished families. Her father, Lieutenant William Herndon, was a naval hero in the ultimate tradition of his service. He had gone down with his ship, the *Central America* in 1857, "dressed in full uniform, standing on the bridge, with indomitable gallantry," ordering his mates away when it became obvious they would drown in a rescue attempt. His conduct had inspired many tributes, among them a monument at the United States Naval Academy and a town house for his widow and daughter on West Twenty-first Street, given by the people of New York.

Soon after she and her mother moved in, Ellen Herndon met Chester Alan Arthur, a promising attorney she found handsome, hearty and socially sophisticated. They fell quickly, deeply in love and were married in October 1859. When the Civil War broke out, Ellen was grateful that her bridegroom, though serving in the state militia, would not face combat. Already a recognised talent in the Republican party, Arthur had been ap-pointed to the governor's military staff and was named brigadier general and quartermaster of New York by April 1862.

The year 1863, however, was one of difficulties and readjustments. Her husband's commission was revoked when a Democrat took over as governor, and Arthur resumed his law practice. Then, in July, their son died. Finding it easier to keep from brooding if she filled her life with many activities, Ellen turned to her music and charity work. She sang for many worthy causes and joined the Mendelssohn Glee Club in 1867. She loved to sing arias by Donizetti, particularly his "Cavatina" from "La Favorita" and "La Mère et l'Enfant."

Domestic tranquility returned with the birth of another son, and later a daughter. At the same time Arthur's career went forward. President Grant had appointed him collector of the Port of New York, a post he held until President Hayes, fighting the spoils system, dismissed him. Then, without warning, Ellen was dead. She never saw her husband attain the vice-presidency, or, after Garfield's death, the presidency.

Indulging his grief for his sweet-faced, Southern wife, Arthur kept her room in their Gramercy Park mansion just as she had left it, placing fresh flowers there each morning. Later, in the White House, he continued his "ritual of remembrance," laying a bouquet beside her photograph each day. Dedicating a stained-glass window to Ellen in St. John's Church, on the south side, where he could see it from the White House, the President brought his lady to Washington, if only in memory.

49

# 22
## Frances Cleveland

### White House Bride

Romantics had waited nearly a century for a president to marry in the White House, and Grover Cleveland obliged them at last in 1886. Asked over the years why he had remained a bachelor, Cleveland had frequently replied, "I'm waiting for my wife to grow up," a comment no one had ever taken seriously. But when the forty-nine-year-old chief executive announced his engagement May 28, 1886, it was obvious he knew for whom he had waited.

She was Frances Folsom, his twenty-one-year-old ward. Her father, Cleveland's law partner, had died in 1875, and "Uncle Cleve " became Frances' guardian. In Buffalo where she lived with her mother, "Uncle Cleve" had become an important man, as sheriff of Erie County and, in 1882, as mayor. Frances was thrilled when he was elected governor of New York, and doubly pleased when he became the Democratic candidate for the presidency in 1884. He was never too busy with politics to take time for "Frank," as he called her, and Frances had no reason to believe his success would in any way change their relationship.

It was Frances' own growing charm and beauty that turned her gruff, middle-aged guardian into a gallant suitor. The burly Cleveland began sending her flowers on every occasion, and invited Frances and her mother to share his box at official presentations. They reached a secret "understanding" while she was at Wells College in Aurora, New York, during which time their meetings were carefully chaperoned by Miss Folsom's mother. The European trip he had arranged after her graduation brought her home to him at last, and, less than a week before the wedding, their engagement was formally announced.

News of the President's romance delighted the nation, which in its excitement over the first White House wedding of a president, cheerfully overlooked the twenty-eight-year age difference of the participants. It was enough that the President had found a bride, and everyone took her to his heart. The Marine Band, led by John Philip Sousa, struck up the *Wedding March* at 7 p.m. June 2, 1886, in the White House. In ivory satin kissed with orange blossoms, Frances Folsom promised to "love...honor, comfort and keep" the President, but not "obey," for Cleveland had insisted the word be omitted from the service. As the newlyweds embraced in the Blue Room, church bells chimed all over Washington, and guns boomed from the Navy Yard.

Cleveland and his bride were not insensitive to the historic aspects of their wedding, but they had valued their privacy more, banning photographers from the ceremony. A private honeymoon was more difficult to arrange, for reporters pursued them to the Maryland mountains, setting up camp as close to their lodge as possible, equipped with telescope, binoculars and cameras.

Before his marriage Cleveland had written to his sister:

I have my heart set upon making Frank a sensible domestic American wife and would be pleased not to hear her spoken of as "The First Lady of the Land" or "The Mistress of the White House." I want her to be happy and possess all she can reasonably desire, but I should feel very much afflicted if she gets many notions in her head. But I think she is pretty level-headed.

Indeed she was. Pleased with her husband's suggestion that they take a private residence near Georgetown where part of the time they could live away from public view, Frances set up housekeeping at "Oak View." When they were in residence in the White House during the social season the Executive Mansion was busier than it had been for decades. At one reception 9,000 people were received, the line weaving all the way to the

50

Treasury Building. She was so gracious that members of her staff found it difficult to keep visitors from slipping back into line for a second smile and handshake. Although she was both young and beautiful, she inspired affection rather than envy for she did not wear décolleté gowns and chose a simple hairstyle. A temperance advocate, she had drunk her own wedding toast in mineral water but did not insist that liquor be banned entirely from her table.

Her popularity was so great that the Republicans used it as a weapon to attack Cleveland with a whispering campaign claiming he beat and abused his lovely wife. Incredulous, Frances ignored the gossip, but when it was charged that she was afraid to speak out, she issued a firm denial. "I can wish the women of our Country no greater blessing than that their home and lives may be as happy, and their husbands may be as kind, attentive, considerate and affectionate as mine." More

damaging to Cleveland was his strong stand for tariff reform and Benjamin Harrison won the election in 1888. Frances moved out of the White House, telling a tearful staff, "Take good care of the house, for we are coming back just four years from today."

And they did. Cleveland's second administration, despite the four-year hiatus, was off to a brilliant start. They were on hand to open the Columbian Exposition in Chicago in 1893, and a White House visit from one of Spain's ruling family set off spectacular celebrations. Then, in the midst of a business panic involving the Silver Purchase Act, the President and his wife faced a crisis that was not revealed until many years later. Cleveland had to undergo surgery for cancer of the mouth. Cleveland, with the help of his wife, kept his illness from the public. The imminent birth of their second child increased the burden for Mrs. Cleveland but universal interest in Esther, born in the White House in September 1893, made it easy to turn the spotlight on the child and away from her father.

After completing their years in the White House the Clevelands retired to Princeton, New Jersey, where the former president died in 1908. Frances continued her educational interests in the University Women's Club, and alumnae work for Wells College. In 1913, five years after Cleveland's death, she married Thomas Preston, Jr., an archaeology professor. World War I found her in charge of the National Security League's Speakers' Bureau and sewing for the needy as president of the Needlework Guild of America. She died in 1947 at the age of eighty-three, still receiving mail from her admirers and requests to address various organizations. She was the beloved First Lady who had left the White House weeping in 1897, saying she was not so much moved by their leaving the presidency as she was by saying goodbye to the surroundings which had become so dear.

# 23
# Caroline Harrison

## A "New Broom"

Although Benjamin Harrison had been elected in 1888 with a homespun "front-porch" campaign spiced with tunes from a *Log Cabin Song Book,* his wife found the White House completely unsatisfactory as a home. Praised as "the best housekeeper that the Pennsylvania Avenue mansion has yet known," Caroline announced she was "very anxious to see the family of the President provided for properly," and launched ambitious plans to "get the present building in good condition."

Congress had quickly thwarted her efforts to build a new residence for the President or begin a drastic renovation of the White House itself, but Caroline was neither discouraged nor defeated. Armed with an appropriation for remodeling, she attacked the Executive Mansion on all levels. Removing layers of flooring, paint and basement dirt, she modernized without destroying the basic aspect of the aging White House. Supervising carefully, even helping with the cleaning, she budgeted well, achieving remarkable results with minimum expenditure.

Caroline was no stranger to running her household with strict economy. She and Ben had been married while he was still a law student, a time when, as a friend pointed out, he was "far from able to support Carrie." But they were very much in love, and Ben worried he would lose her if he waited until he was "laden with yellow gold." They had already waited some time, for their romance began when Carrie was fifteen and Ben, nearly a year younger, was a student at Farmers' College. Caroline's father, the Reverend John Witherspoon Scott, taught there for a while, then moved with his family to Oxford, Ohio, where he founded the Oxford Female Institute. Not long afterward Ben chose to finish his education at Miami University in Oxford so that he could be near his "charming and loveable" Carrie.

They were married in 1853 when Carrie was twenty-one. Ben took her first to North Bend, Indiana, where he had been raised by his parents and grandmother, Anna Symmes Harrison. Later they moved to Indianapolis, living in a boardinghouse while Ben worked as a court crier before his legal practice took hold.

Separated by the Civil War, Carrie raised her son and daughter alone, finding fellowship and diversion through her church, the First Presbyterian. She taught needlework and china painting to many of its members, worked for the missionary society and became a well-liked Sunday school teacher. When Ben returned he found his wife's innate friendliness and creative talents had won for her almost as much popularity as he himself had achieved. The Civil War, it seemed, had done nearly as much for him as the Indian up-

WHITE HOUSE COLLECTION

Mrs. Benjamin Harrison's plan to enlarge
the crowded Executive Mansion called for
elaborate wings and a greenhouse.

LIBRARY OF CONGRESS

risings had for his grandfather, William Henry Harrison. Returning to Indianapolis in 1865 with an enviable reputation as a leader and fighting brigadier general, Ben plunged into politics. Joining the Republicans, he ran unsuccessfully for governor, then was elected to the Senate in 1881.

Caroline was sorry that their arrival in Washington coincided with the departure of Rutherford and Lucy Hayes, whom she had entertained in Indiana in 1879. Ben had once told Caroline, "If my ambition is to soar.... you will have to give it wings," and she had done just that. Her Hoosier warmth was one of his most valuable political assets, even in Washington where she adopted the Capital's more formal customs without sacrificing her midwestern friendliness. Ben, by contrast, was so cold and aloof it was said, "If you prick him, he would bleed ice water." Nevertheless, he was nominated for the presidency in 1889, winning an electoral victory, although losing the popular vote to Grover Cleveland.

Caroline's complaints about conditions in the White House were justified, particularly considering the size of her family. The mansion's five bedrooms and one bath nearly overflowed with Harrisons, including Dr. Scott, Caroline's elderly father, Mary Scott Dimmick, her widowed niece, her son and daughter, their mates and assorted grandchildren. Although Caroline managed nicely when the remodeling was completed, she regretted that Congress had rejected all three plans for expansion which she had submitted.

Caroline wasted no time getting her ménage under control. After an eight o'clock breakfast and half-hour prayer service, she began her daily household inspection. It was said that no dusty corner escaped her eye, particularly since electricity had been installed, considerably improving illumination. This modern marvel, however, intimidated Caroline and her family. They preferred to let the lights burn all night rather than turn them off and risk getting a shock.

With customary zeal, Caroline undertook another project inspired during the White House modernization. Removing an old china closet, she began sorting and identifying dinnerware from previous administrations, forming the basis of the White House china collection.

During Harrison's term of office, the White House actually became the "garden spot of orchids" Julia Grant had spoken of years before. Caroline loved orchids and filled the conservatory with their lavender blooms. She even painted a "White House orchid," dedicating it to "mothers, wives, and daughters of America." In 1890, when she was named the first president general of the Daughters of the American Revolution, her fondness for the flower inspired its use as the organization's traditional corsage.

Another tradition also had its roots in the Harrison administration. Caroline had the first White House Christmas tree put up in the upstairs Oval Room, where it was decorated by virtually everyone in the Executive Mansion: the President, his family and the entire staff.

Then, during the last year of her husband's term, Caroline was stricken, probably with tuberculosis, and died in the White House October 25, 1892. As her body lay in state in the East Room, Benjamin lost all desire for reelection. He did not campaign and seemed grateful to hand his office back to Grover Cleveland in 1893.

Three and a half years later he married his wife's niece, Mary Scott Dimmick, who had been with him and Caroline in the White House. He died in 1901, leaving his second wife with a young daughter, Elizabeth. Before her own death in 1948, Mary Dimmick Harrison established The Benjamin Harrison Memorial Home in Indianapolis, Indiana.

# 24
## Ida McKinley

THE WESTERN RESERVE HISTORICAL SOCIETY

### Beloved Invalid

Few people noticed that Ida McKinley had collapsed at her husband's Inaugural Ball March 4, 1897, for the President, supporting his invalid wife, whisked her quickly away when she fainted. But collectors at the Smithsonian Institution, receiving her exquisite blue and silver ball gown, saw the "mark or stain on the satin where she fell."

Only close friends realized that the new First Lady was an epileptic, an affliction never acknowledged by the President. They did not reveal the nature of her illness for Ida wanted desperately to share as much of William's life as possible, and public awareness of her condition would have made this even more difficult. Most people in the Capital knew only that Mrs. McKinley suffered from a nervous disorder which made it necessary for her to receive while seated, clutching a bouquet to discourage handshakes.

To William McKinley this withered woman was still "the most beautiful girl you ever saw." It had been love at first sight between him and vivacious Ida Saxton, a blooming finishing-school product recently home from a European tour. They met in her hometown, Canton, Ohio, where Major McKinley settled after the Civil War. The young attorney found Ida different from any girl he had ever known for, in addition to being pretty and popular, she had made a small place for herself in the banking profession. Her father, James Saxton, was a Canton banker who trained his daughter in his business. She loved her work, eventually earning a promotion to cashier.

When she and William were married in January 1871, Ida stopped work and looked forward to happy years raising her daughters, Katherine and Ida, who were born in 1871 and 1873. Childbirth complications, however, left Ida with recurring convulsions. She could not walk again without assistance and required constant care. Then baby Ida died, followed some time later by little Katherine, leaving their mother shattered in mind and body.

Their family gone, Ida and William turned to one another with even more affection and devotion than before. An invalid wife was certainly a liability to William as he sought a career in public office, but he never neglected her. He took her with him to Washington when he served in Congress from 1877 to 1891, and later, as governor of Ohio, chose a hotel across from the Capitol for their residence. He could see Ida from his office window and waved to her each day, returning in the evening with fresh roses for her room. There was little Ida could do for him other than fashion his flat satin bow ties which became something of a McKinley trademark.

As president, William McKinley coped with Ida's illness by changing protocol so she could sit next to him at state dinners. Meanwhile he wrestled with decisions regarding war with Spain in the aftermath of the loss of the *Maine* in Havana harbor. Even during the most difficult days he was solicitous of his wife, for Ida participated in as many state functions as possible and insisted on accompanying William on most trips.

She had accompanied him to Buffalo, New York, where on September 7, 1901, he was shot by a young anarchist. Resting at the home of the president of the Buffalo Exposition, she learned of the tragedy. The dying president's thoughts were for Ida. "My wife— be careful. . .how you tell her—oh, be careful." She died six years later, having wished for death to come. "Why should I linger? Please God, if it is Thy will, let me go. I want to be with him."

# 25
## Alice Roosevelt

HARVARD COLLEGE LIBRARY

### T. R.'s "Sunshine"

"I first saw her on October 18, 1878, and loved her as soon as I saw her sweet, fair young face," wrote Theodore Roosevelt, captivated in his junior year at Harvard by a seventeen-year-old girl who had invaded his life and dreams. She was Alice Hathaway Lee, the daughter of eminent Bostonian George Cabot Lee, a "laughing, pretty little witch," who was singularly unimpressed with Theodore's sudden ardent courtship.

But Alice, so consistently easy-going and cheerful her friends called her "Sunshine," could not adequately discourage her irrepressible suitor. During a party at the Hasty Pudding Club he pointed to her and declared, "See that girl? I'm going to marry her. She won't have me but I am going to have *her!*" Recalling that her sister's romance with Theodore was at first completely one-sided, Rose Lee commented that Alice "had no intention of marrying him—but she did!"

She turned down his first proposal at the end of his junior year, but during the first part of his senior year, her indecision had worked Theodore up to a state of frequent sleepless wandering in the woods near Cambridge. Finally, unable to stand it any longer, he went to her home "determined to make an end of things at last . . . after much pleading, my sweet, pretty darling consented to be my wife."

They were married October 27, 1880, at a gala ceremony well-attended by Roosevelts and by the girl some of the family had expected him to marry, Edith Kermit Carow. During their honeymoon at Tranquility, the Roosevelt Oyster Bay estate, they climbed nearby Sagamore Hill. Loving its magnificent hilltop view of Long Island, they schemed to buy it for their future home, envisioning a large piazza "where we could sit in rocking chairs and watch the sunset."

In the spring, after Theodore finished a year at Columbia Law School, he and Alice took a trip to Europe. While in Switzerland, Alice waited fearfully in her hotel room while Theodore scaled the Matterhorn, although she had pleaded with him not to attempt the climb.

Alice was well aware that her husband's decisions could seldom be influenced by herself or others, and she quickly learned to keep up with him as best she could, rather than oppose him. The rest of his family, however, were disturbed by his desire to enter politics at the lowest level—as a precinct worker. His quick election to the state assembly, however, was well received, and Alice was pleased when he was praised as a courageous, outspoken reformer.

During his second term in the assembly they did not take rooms in Albany, as they had done before, because Alice was expecting a baby, and Theodore was anxious for her to have every comfort. He moved her into his mother's house on Fifty-Seventh Street, where she waited happily for the birth of "Princess Alice." In Albany, Theodore received a welcome telegram announcing the arrival of a daughter, followed by a second stating his wife's condition was giving cause for alarm. Reaching home, he found Alice barely conscious, although their little baby girl was doing well. An apparent victim of Bright's disease, Alice did not rally. After her death February 14, 1884, Theodore wrote, "when my heart's dearest died, the light went from my life forever." Theodore Roosevelt, dealt another heavy blow that same day with the death of his mother, left the East to try to forget his grief in the untamed West. He never mentioned his "Sunshine" again.

55

# 26
## Edith Roosevelt

### Second Wife, First Lady

PAINTING BY THEOBALD CHARTRAN, WHITE HOUSE COLLECTION

"President McKinley died at 2:15 this morning. Theodore Roosevelt." Reading the telegram at their Adirondack retreat, Edith Roosevelt was deceived neither by the terseness of the message nor the formality of her husband's signature. He was no longer McKinley's reluctant vice-president, but President of the United States. Their place was now in Washington. Ten days later, they moved into the White House.

Like Theodore, Edith refused to dwell on the tragedy which had given him the presidency, although she knew he carried a revolver in public to "have some chance of shooting the assassin before he could shoot me." T.R. took an optimistic view of his own future. Upon moving into the White House on the day of his late father's birthday he said it seemed, "as if there were a special blessing on the life I am to live here."

The woman who shared his life in the White House was not the love of his college days, his first wife, Alice, but Edith Carow

Roosevelt, a dear childhood companion who had long been a part of his life. He had reached out to Edith two years after Alice's death, though he berated himself for doing so crying, "I have no constancy!" But "Dear Eidie," the girl T.R. had written lonesome letters to when he was eleven, drew him to her even across the Atlantic. Traveling to London, where she had moved with her widowed mother, T.R. married her there in December 1886, admitting to himself "the greatest privilege and duty for any man is to be happily married."

His bride endorsed "the strenuous life" as heartily as he. Together they climbed mountains, rode horseback, sailed, or rowed for hours. She shared his passion for reading, to his delight. Years before, however, at Miss Comstock's school, Edith's classmates had criticized her for being too bookish. At Sagamore Hill, a many-chimneyed hive of literary, political and physical activity, Edith raised Alice, the daughter of Theodore's first wife, and their own family of four boys and a girl.

Edith never knew what to expect next of her rampaging husband. As police commissioner of New York, his lively exploits were a constant source of cartoons and controversy, and she had reason to believe he would cause similar commotion as McKinley's Assistant Secretary of the Navy. She was right. Taking advantage of the absence of his superior, T.R. cabled orders to Admiral Dewey to prepare for possible war with Spain. After the sinking of the *Maine,* T.R. left Washington to fight the Spaniards in the field with a rowdy regiment of Rough Riders.

Victory at San Juan Hill, however, turned Roosevelt into a national celebrity and popular candidate for governor of New York. Edith, with the rest of the family, stood firmly behind him during the campaign. As always she offered quiet advice which he sometimes followed, though he admitted "Whenever I go

56

THEODORE ROOSEVELT ASSOCIATION

This rambling, many-gabled house on Sagamore Hill rang with the robust living of T. R. and his vigorous family.

against her judgment I regret it." On occasion she became particularly concerned with his attacks on political opponents. She strongly urged caution and moderation when she felt T.R.'s charges were becoming too personal.

Edith had enjoyed those days in public service very much. T.R. had commented that when he was civil service commissioner, she "never minded our not having champagne at our dinners." She successfully did most of her entertaining at a Sunday evening high tea. Later at the White House, she turned mere receptions into musicales, bringing culture and conviviality together.

As governor T.R. had said, "Walk softly and carry a big stick," a maxim Edith knew he seldom adhered to, for the echo of his Rough Riders' boots could be heard everywhere. The men he had led to victory in Cuba were fiercely loyal to him, and T.R., in turn, helped them, finding them jobs and even, on occasion, bailing them out of jail. Edith felt a certain responsibility toward them and was everlastingly patient with her Rough Rider charges. She admitted, however, that she and Theodore were like "the parents of a thousand very large and bad children."

Edith shared her husband's schemes as well as his dreams. Perhaps only she knew whether he wore his Rough Rider hat to the Republican convention in 1900 to hide a bandage on his head or to spark enthusiasm for his nomination as vice-president. He was publicly reluctant to accept the second spot, but she knew he would accept if sincere national sentiment were shown on his behalf.

Then McKinley's assassination brought to the presidency the youngest man to serve in the office. To a White House long infused with melancholy and illness came an irrepressible family whose escapades delighted the nation. Edith was in charge of six children and pets by the score, both domestic and exotic, including a pony the children brought up to their rooms in the mansion's elevator. T.R.'s major White House renovation hit a snag when his children's roller-skating on the newly-laid East Room floor damaged the wood. The White House at last became the official name of the Executive Mansion when Theodore had "White House" inscribed on his stationery and Edith's invitations. The social highlight of Roosevelt's administration was the wedding of his first wife's daughter, "Princess Alice," to Congressman Nicholas Longworth in 1906.

Turning the presidency over to his friend Will Taft in 1909, T.R. gleefully embarked on an African trip. He had left Edith behind but rejoiced at their reunion in Egypt and subsequent world tour. "Catch me ever leaving her for a year again!" he exclaimed.

Edith felt deeply for her husband when his friendship with Taft deteriorated. She remembered when they were together at the White House, laughing so hard they could be heard even from behind closed doors. She knew he had thought carefully before opposing his former friend in the election of 1912. Receiving more votes than Taft was small consolation in the bitterness of the contest which Wilson won.

Sagamore Hill seemed strangely quiet with their children grown, and quieter still when their youngest son, Quentin, died in World War I. After her husband's death in 1919, Edith recalled he "spoke of the happiness of being home and made little plans for me."

She never divulged those plans, but not long afterward she embarked on her "Odyssey of a Grandmother," finding comfort in travel. In speaking of happier times she recalled that "no family ever enjoyed the White House more than we." Two more sons died before Edith's own death in 1948. Refusing to bow to grief, she had immersed herself in work for the Republican party. There, as always, hers was a soft voice, never a bugle.

# 27
## Helen Taft

### Cherry Blossom Legacy

Watching her husband take the oath of office in the Senate chamber March 4, 1909, Helen Taft felt "inexpressibly happy." Admitting that "it has always been my ambition to see Mr. Taft President of the United States," she shared his triumph that day in a way no First Lady ever had. With great personal satisfaction she settled herself in his carriage for the post-Inaugural ride down Pennsylvania Avenue, delighted that since former President Roosevelt had already left Washington she had the place of honor on Taft's left.

Her arrival at the White House fulfilled another one of her ambitions, one of even longer standing than her wish to see Mr. Taft president. During Rutherford Hayes' administration when Helen was seventeen, she had been a guest at the Executive Mansion. Life there so impressed her that she had declared she would only be satisfied to marry a man who could take her there, and her "adorable Will Taft" became that man.

As for Helen, she was the woman *The Washington Post* had called "In the matter of mental attainments. . . .probably the best-fitted woman who ever graced the position she now holds and enjoys." To the public, the new President and his lady seemed an indomitable couple.

They had met at a coasting party on a snow-crusted hill outside of Cincinnati when Helen was eighteen. Later, Taft liked to joke that she shared his bobsled then "and Nellie and I have been sliding downhill ever since." But Helen Herron saw anything but a downhill course for her ample, good-natured beau. He had graduated second in his class at Yale and was already making a brilliant reputation for himself as an attorney when he and Helen were married in June 1886.

Although the daughter of a judge, Helen considered a career on the bench "quite too settled." Will himself longed for the judicial life but had great respect for his wife's opinions. A former teacher, she was both intelligent and articulate. Before their marriage she had organized a "salon" to foster "brilliant discussion of topics intellectual and economic." Will had enjoyed these sessions where he became aware of Helen's considerable intellect and admitted that he, more than anyone, admired her "powers of reasoning."

The political career she wanted for Will was not long in coming. He went to Washington in 1890 as U.S. Solicitor General, returning to Ohio two years later when President Harrison appointed him to a federal judgeship. During this time Helen helped to establish the Cincinnati Symphony Orchestra renewing an earlier interest in music.

Then, in an unexpected move, President McKinley sent Will to the Philippines as head of the commission to govern the islands. Knowing she "didn't want to miss a big and novel experience," Helen and her three children went along. She reveled in the attention she received when he became the first American civil governor. She adapted herself quickly to life in the East, though she kept an American garden, her own cow and chickens at the Malacañan Palace.

Helen was concerned when the new President, Theodore Roosevelt, offered Will an appointment to the Supreme Court for she knew that such a move would eliminate her husband from the presidency. He declined, however, on the grounds he could not leave the Filipinos until they were more nearly self-sustaining. But later, an appointment as T.R.'s Secretary of War met with Helen's approval. "It was in line with the kind of work I wanted my husband to do, the kind of career I wanted for him and expected him to have," she said. She was less philosophic about the inadequate salary of a cabinet officer, however, commenting, "I thought what a curious and peculiarly American sort of promotion it was which carried with it such diminished advantages."

58

In Washington her ambition for her husband was within reach. She had only to convince Will he should not accept the next appointment to the Supreme Court and to persuade Roosevelt that Taft was the only man to succeed him as president. One evening at the White House T.R. said, half in jest, he could see something hanging over Taft's head. "At one time it looks like the presidency," he said. "Then again it looks like the chief justiceship!"

"Make it the chief justiceship," Taft responded.

"Make it the presidency," insisted Helen.

She met with Roosevelt privately to discuss her husband's future. Observers at the White House noted, "Mrs. Taft, in the face of opposition of both the President and her husband carried her point. From that time on, the President seemed to feel Mr. Taft should be his successor."

Once elected president, Taft felt T.R.'s mantle weighed heavily, even on his stout shoulders. The rift in their friendship widened when Taft dismissed Roosevelt appointees. Helen had foreseen the split, and when T.R. opposed Taft for the Republican nomination in 1912, she reminded Will of her mistrust of Roosevelt. Taft responded, "I think you are perfectly happy now. You would have preferred the Colonel to come out against me than to have been wrong yourself."

Early in Taft's administration Helen Taft suffered a stroke which for a time left her without full use of her faculties. She learned to talk again with her husband's help, although her speech remained somewhat impaired. Afterwards she gave domestic affairs her full attention, claiming, " My very active participation in my husband's career came to an end when he became president." This, of course, was not entirely the case. She kept records of Taft's important appointments for him and monitored most White House con-

PAINTING BY BROR KRONSTRAND, WHITE HOUSE COLLECTION

ferences. She always offered him advice, which he frequently took.

Mrs. Taft's precedent-breaking drive to the White House after the Inauguration was not her only innovation as First Lady. She replaced the mansion's police guard with Negro servants in livery and arranged musicales following state dinners. These changes drew criticism, but another plan was an unqualified success. Deciding to enhance Potomac Park with cherry blossoms, like those she had seen years before in Japan, she talked Tokyo's Mayor Ozaki into giving 3,000 trees to the Capital.

When the Tafts left the White House in 1913 after Wilson's victory the trees had not yet bloomed. But, returning to Washington eight years later when Will became chief justice and remaining there after his death in 1930, Helen Taft saw the pink profusion of yet another dream come true each spring until her death in 1943.

59

# 28
## Ellen Wilson

### "An Angel in the White House"

From her seat on the portico of the Capitol Ellen Wilson watched Woodrow kiss her own small Bible as the chief justice held it open before him. Then, too moved by his Inaugural address to remain in her place, she slipped through the crowd to stand directly beneath the platform, beaming up at him as he spoke, "This is not a day of triumph; it is a day of dedication."

The new First Lady was as committed to the solemnity of the occasion as her husband, and at their request, plans for an Inaugural Ball had been cancelled. The Wilsons, both children of Presbyterian ministers, felt the customary gala was not only frivolous but inappropriate. Instead the evening of March 4, 1913, was spent in their new residence with their happy, close-knit family. The President himself left the White House only briefly to visit with some Princeton students before returning to his wife and three daughters.

Ellen frankly adored her husband, whose affection for her was equally obvious. With her he was never the dry, pedantic man he seemed in public but a tender, still-romantic husband. He never really got over the fact that pretty Ellie Lou Axson, the girl "with hair like burnished copper," had agreed to be his wife. He had courted the drawling Georgia miss from the moment he first noticed her one morning in church, and his love letters did not stop with their marriage in June 1885. Over the years they exchanged some 1,400 love notes, written during every separation.

Sharing the academic life with Woodrow at Bryn Mawr, Wesleyan and Princeton, Ellen sometimes felt her own education at Georgia's Shorter College had been inadequate. Woodrow, however, delighted in the fact that she was "receptive not aggressive." He said, "A man could read her a treatise or a long essay and would never interrupt until the end—she had what I call a speaking silence." She also had a great deal of artistic talent and was a trained, accomplished painter, having studied at the Art Students League of New York. Even in the White House she was seldom away from her easel. Ellen sold many of her paintings for charity, and even those donated anonymously brought good prices.

As First Lady her Georgia gentlewoman's graciousness charmed everyone. She had told her husband, "Since you have married someone who is not gay, I must provide for you friends who are," encouraging the visits of scintillating men and women. With a Southerner's gift for warm, unstilted hospitality, she entertained frequently in the garden, pouring tea and offering home-baked delicacies.

She did not, however, feel that her first responsibility as First Lady was to entertain. "I think we have an angel in the White House," said one of her staff. "She is talking about the poor and improving the housing." Ellen did more than talk. She visited the Capital's slums and, appalled by conditions there, prodded congressmen to draft housing legislation. Disappointed when the House was slow to act, she continued to help the poor with food and money. She devoted much time to other philanthropies as well, encouraging her daughters, Margaret, Jessie and Eleanor, to do the same.

Then, in the spring of 1914, Ellen fell gravely ill. News of war in Europe was withheld from her, at Woodrow's insistence, but she remained deeply concerned with the future of her slum clearance project. Finally, realizing the First Lady was near death, Congress at last passed the housing legislation she had inspired. Hearing the news, she could only smile and touch her husband's hand.

Ellen had said, "I wonder how anyone who reaches middle age can bear it, if she cannot feel, on looking back. . .she has on the whole lived for others and not for herself." When she died of Bright's disease August 6, 1914, no one doubted she had lived unselfishly.

60

# 29
## Edith Wilson

### First Lady or Acting President

PAINTING OF EDITH WILSON BY MÜLLER-URY,
WHITE HOUSE COLLECTION

DETAIL FROM PAINTING OF ELLEN WILSON BY ROBERT VONNAH,
THE WOODROW WILSON HOUSE

Edith Galt stepped out of the White House elevator and almost into President Wilson's arms. "Cousin Woodrow," chuckled her companion, Helen Bones, "I should like to present Mrs. Norman Galt." Delighted that his early return with Dr. Cary Grayson, White House physician, from a round of golf had resulted in such a pleasant, if unexpected encounter, Wilson insisted the violet-eyed widow join him for tea. Nine months later they were married. Edith had, as she said, "turned a corner and met my fate," a fate that affected not only her future and Wilson's but that of the entire nation during a critical period.

Edith Wilson, perhaps the most controversial First Lady, was a ninth-generation direct descendant of Pocahontas, the Indian princess, and John Rolfe. Her proud Southern family held lands near Appomattox for generations until forced to abandon them after the Civil War. Then Edith's father, William Bolling, became a circuit-court judge, raising his nine children in Wytheville, Virginia.

Financial considerations curtailed Edith's education, and, after two years of college, she was sent to visit her sister in Washington, D.C. There she met and married Norman Galt, a member of the family-held jewelry firm from which Thomas Jefferson had purchased the White House silver service. The store's reputation had grown with the years, and, when Norman died suddenly in 1908, Edith was left a well-to-do widow. She had no children but enjoyed young friends like Wilson's cousin, Helen Bones.

It was soon apparent after the meeting at the White House elevator that another Southerner would become mistress of the Executive Mansion, but fond memories of Ellen Wilson kept some from endorsing Wilson's pursuit of Mrs. Galt. Most people, particularly his family, were happy to see him shake off the gloom that had enveloped him since Ellen's death in August 1914.

Meanwhile, Edith feared that part of her attraction to Wilson might have been the glory of his office. She said, "If you are defeated for election next year I'll marry you," but she changed her mind and accepted his proposal when she realized how strong her own feelings had become. Some of Wilson's advisors, wild at the thought of his remarriage, told him that an old scandal would be revived and that Edith's name as well as his own would be muddied. Ashen, Wilson told Edith he would release her from her promise to marry him, but she responded, "I am not afraid of gossip or threat with your love as my shield."

They were married December 18, 1915, at Edith's home. Next morning, a startled secret service man encountered the top-hatted bridegroom prancing down the honeymoon train in his cutaway whistling "Oh, you beautiful doll." At the White House, the staff found the new First Lady "a blessing and a delight to President Wilson." She saw to it that he played Dr. Grayson's prescribed round of golf before breakfast, later riding horseback with him when the pressures of war left insufficient time for golf.

When Wilson taught her his secret code for communicating with emissaries abroad, she took part in an even more important part of his life. Edith was soon transcribing his messages and decoding the incoming cables as well. Late one night, when five messages were received by the President, he said, "These are your work, Edith, so there is no rest in sight for either of us."

Despite a strong challenge by Republican Charles Evans Hughes, Wilson was reelected in 1916. Edith, who was opposed to women's suffrage, seemed undismayed that she could not vote, though she expected Wilson to lose. She called picketing suffragettes "detestable" and even admitted Wilson's address at a suffrage meeting was "the only speech of my Precious One I ever failed to enjoy."

Though reelected with the slogan "He kept us out of war," Wilson abandoned neutrality when Germany continued to sink American ships and submarines. Promising to "make the world safe for democracy," he asked Congress to declare war April 2, 1917. Four days later, when the declaration reached his desk, Edith asked, "Please use the pen you gave me." With a stroke of Edith's pen, we were at war.

Determined to set the proper example in running a wartime household, even in the White House, Edith observed Food Administrator Hoover's "wheatless and meatless days" as well as heatless days and gasless Sundays, walking to church or riding in an old horse-drawn carriage. Her sewing machine, one of the few items she had brought to the White House as a bride, became a humming hub for Red Cross work, and she sewed by the hour. The sheep grazing on the White House lawn saved man-hours by keeping the grass short, and their wool, when sold, provided nearly $100,000 for the Red Cross.

Traveling with Woodrow to Europe in January 1919, Edith shared the jubilation of peace. Hidden in an antechamber at the Peace Conference, which no women were allowed to attend, she heard Wilson speak passionately on behalf of the League of Nations, the most vital of his Fourteen Points, and saw the delegates unanimously approve his proposal. However, the United States Senate balked at ratifying the Covenant of the League. Taking his case to the public, Wilson, despite his failing health, undertook a whistle-stop tour hoping to sell the League to the American people. Suddenly one night he called to Edith, "I'm terribly sick," and she saw one side of his face had crumpled strangely. From then on she knew "life would never be the same . . . from that hour on I would have to wear a mask— not only to the public but to the one I loved . . . for he must never know how ill he was, and I must carry on."

LIBRARY OF CONGRESS

Grazing sheep on the White House lawn released men for the war effort of 1917-18.

And carry on she did, exercising an authority unparalleled by any First Lady, while her husband lay paralyzed from a second, far more severe stroke suffered at the White House in October. Dr. Grayson and a panel of consulting specialists agreed that despite his paralysis, the President's mind was "clear as crystal." Convinced that "he can still do more with a maimed body than anyone else," they urged Edith to "have everything come to you. Weigh the importance of each matter and see if it is possible to solve it by consultation with the head of the department involved without your husband's advice."

"So," wrote Mrs. Wilson, "began my stewardship." Others called it "Mrs. Wilson's Regency," vilifying her in the press as "Acting President," "Mrs. President," or even "Secretary to the President and Acting Secretary of State." She bore such criticism stoically, insisting, "I, myself, never made a single decision regarding the disposition of public affairs. The only decision that was mine was what was important and what was not." This, of course, was a decision of some magnitude, one that would normally have been made by cabinet-level officials.

Their hands, however, were tied. Edith and the physicians had effectively limited their access to the President. Moreover, the doctors made it clear any attempt to force them to declare the President incompetent would fail. Dr. Grayson, learning such a move was afoot, said, "I shall testify that the President is completely competent to perform the duties of the office." The doctors rebuffed even Edith's suggestion that Wilson resign, saying depriving him of his job would remove his incentive to live, and would be neither in his best interests nor the nation's.

Though historians disagree as to how long Edith Wilson held the reigns of government, she herself claimed her "stewardship" lasted only six weeks. It was true that after his stroke on October 2 no one but Edith and his doctors saw him for several weeks, but on October 30 the king and queen of Belgium visited with the invalid and found him recuperating nicely. By mid-November he was seen in his wheelchair on the south portico, and his December 3 message to Congress was said to be unmistakably his own work. It was February, however, before he received Secretary of State Lansing and April when cabinet meetings were resumed. Rumors that the President was dying or insane had persisted, and many felt Edith's role as political arbiter continued for many months, if not until the end of his term.

He retired a broken man when the public decisively defeated the Democrats and Wilson's "great and solemn referendum on the League," electing Warren G. Harding by a landslide. Edith nursed him devotedly until his death in 1924, then took up what she called her "Cause," honoring his memory whenever and wherever possible. An active director of the Woodrow Wilson Foundation, she even traveled to Poland for the unveiling of a statue of her husband. An ardent Democrat, she was herself honored by succeeding administrations. At the Inauguration of John F. Kennedy she occupied a special seat almost directly behind the President.

When she died in December 1961, at the age of eighty-nine, the extent of her influence on the President and hence on the nation at the time of her illness was still in dispute. The situation she had faced could, in fact, have occurred again, for it was not until 1967 that the twenty-fifth amendment to the Constitution, "Presidential Disability and Succession," became law. Whatever part she played in history, her motives were clearly those of a wife, not a monarch. "Woodrow Wilson was first my beloved husband whose life I was trying to save," she said. "After that he was President of the United States."

# 30
## Florence Harding

### "The Duchess"

Florence Harding eagerly followed her husband up the steps of the Capitol, sweeping past invalid President Wilson who could not negotiate the stairs. It was March 4, 1921, and "The Duchess" could hardly wait for her husband to take the oath of office. "Well, Warren Harding, I have got you the Presidency," she had said when she learned he had been elected. "What are you going to do with it?"

"Return to normalcy" had been his campaign promise, and it was one the American people had heartily endorsed by giving him a landslide victory at the polls. "Normalcy," however, meant different things to different people, and Harding's own version caused problems from the outset. The "plain folks" midwestern image the Hardings had projected during the campaign blurred quickly. They had tried to resume the custom of a great Inaugural parade and Ball, but gave up their plans when criticism became intense. To the general public, it was unbecoming ostentation for a nation emerging from the deprivation of World War I.

Feeling that her husband's administration had gotten off to a slow social start, Florence threw open the gates of the White House, embarking on a full schedule of receptions and handshakes. She welcomed everyone, tourists as well as politicians. "It's their White House," she quipped. "Let them look in if they want to." The lawn erupted in a rash of garden parties and the smartly tailored First Lady visited hospitals and other institutions.

Although she took as great a part as did her husband in the "smoke-filled-room" poker sessions in the White House, defying Prohibition and mixing drinks for "Ohio Gang" cronies, the newspapers were kind to the new First Lady, touting for some time her abilities as a hostess. She had, after all, been a newspaperwoman herself. In 1891 when she married Harding in Marion, Ohio, he was pub-

LIBRARY OF CONGRESS

lisher of the *Star*. Not long after their wedding he became ill, and she went down to his office "temporarily to help out." She stayed fourteen years. In the evenings she bicycled home half an hour early to cook Warren's dinner, then helped formulate his speeches for a growing schedule of public appearances. Florence's virtual "take-over" at the *Star* freed Warren to pursue the political career both craved for him, and he went quickly from state senator to lieutenant governor and United States senator.

Florence had said, "I have only one real hobby—it's my husband," and no one doubted the truth of her words. She knew that the way to hold Warren, despite his frequent romantic entanglements, was to "always have reserve food in the icebox and never let my husband travel without me." Her first marriage, a teen-age elopement, had ended in divorce, and she had no intention of losing Warren. Deserted by her first husband, Henry

DeWolfe, and left with an infant son, Florence had supported herself by borrowing a piano and giving lessons. She was a talented musician and accomplished pianist, having attended the Cincinnati Conservatory of Music before her marriage.

Florence's father, Amos Kling, a wealthy banker in Marion, refused to help his struggling daughter, though he adopted his grandson. He bitterly opposed her romance with Harding, five years her junior, because he felt Harding was her social inferior. He believed persistent rumors that Harding was part Negro and, after the marriage, did not speak to his daughter for seven years.

Such a background had apparently inured Florence to family strife, for she concentrated on Warren's career, not their domestic relations. His liaison with a friend's wife was well-known in Marion, and in the White House he was reported to have dallied with a woman almost under Florence's nose. There was evidence, to be sure, as White House Chief Usher Ike Hoover said, that "Harding was a sporting ladies' man."

Poker-playing, fun-loving Harding may have "looked like a President," but he seldom acted like one. When elected, he said, "I have lost my freedom," regretting that he had allowed Florence and political boss Harry Daugherty to push him into the presidency. Florence, however, continued to take an active part in his policy making, often without his knowledge. She conferred with cabinet officials on her own, leaving Harding to wonder where she got so much inside information.

Late in 1922 rumors of corruption of Harding subordinates began to circulate in Washington and upset the lax atmosphere of politics and poker. Florence had often said that Warren did well when he followed her advice and poorly when he did not, but scandal tainted her appointees as well as his, notably Charles Forbes of the Veterans Bureau. A mounting tally of bribery, blackmail and graft resulted in several suicides and one possible murder. The "Ohio Gang" had betrayed them badly.

Rumblings of what would later be the Teapot Dome scandal and a setback in Congress goaded the President into making a cross-country "Voyage of Understanding" to restore his public image. Perhaps the Hardings hoped the trip would relieve some of their domestic strain as well. Neither had been well in past months. Beneath Florence's marcelled façade and glittering pince-nez was an aging, very sick woman. Chronic kidney trouble had sapped her strength. The trip, which began in June 1923, seemed like a welcome diversion to the troubled couple.

But the news from Washington which caught up with their speeding train was as bad as that from which they had fled. "In this job I am not worried about my enemies. It is my friends who are keeping me awake nights," muttered Harding. On returning from Alaska, Harding collapsed and on August 2 while in San Francisco he died, probably of a blood clot on the brain, while Florence was reading him a favorable magazine article, "A Calm View of a Calm Man."

The presidential train, the *Superb,* became a funeral cortege. Nearly a week later, when Harding's body lay in state in the East Room, Florence said, "No one can hurt you now, Warren." Coolly, methodically, she burned virtually all his papers, leaving his part and hers in the corruption riddled administration forever open to speculation. When she died in November 1924, having seen his name become synonymous with scandal, many people remembered what she had said when Harding received the presidential nomination. Ruefully, despite her own ambition for him, she had commented, "I can see but one word written over his head if they make him President, and that is tragedy."

65

# 31
## Grace Coolidge

### "Fire, Spirit and Dew"

PAINTING BY HOWARD CHANDLER CHRISTY,
WHITE HOUSE COLLECTION

At the Coolidge farmhouse, in the sultry darkness of the summer night, Grace Coolidge carefully arranged the family Bible and a kerosene lamp in the center of the parlor table. Minutes later, at 2:47 a.m., August 3, 1923, she watched her husband sworn in as President of the United States.

Details of the "Lamplight Inaugural" in Plymouth Notch, Vermont, intrigued the American public, and the wholesome New England couple who moved into the White House charmed them. Vice-president and Mrs. Coolidge had lived modestly at Willard's Hotel, feeling they could not afford a home in the Capital. Florence Harding, effectively squelching a move to purchase a mansion as a permanent residence for the vice-president, had said, "I just couldn't have people like those Coolidges living in that beautiful house," then stood by helplessly when Harding's death thrust "those Coolidges" into the White House.

The new First Lady, a native of Burlington, Vermont, was a Yankee like her husband, but as outgoing as Cal was taciturn. Warm and engaging, friends called Grace a "creature of fire, spirit and dew." She had said, "People are my books," quoting from a popular song " 'the short, the fat, the lean, the tall; I don't give a rap, I love them all.' " No one doubted her sincerity. As a teacher of handicapped children she had for years demonstrated her concern for others. In Northampton, Massachusetts, where she taught at the Clarke Institute for the Deaf, she was regarded as a sensitive teacher and community-minded young woman. There, in 1903, she met Calvin Coolidge. He courted Grace Goodhue, his first and only love, for two years before they were married October 4, 1905. She remained in Northampton while "Silent Cal" combined law with politics and rose from city councilman to governor of Massachusetts.

Calvin's advisors openly regarded Grace as his most valuable political asset. One of them commented, "She will make friends wherever she goes, and she will not meddle with his conduct of the office." Grace, who adored her laconic husband, had no intention of interfering with his politics. A natural campaigner, she said she loved meeting people and was delighted that Cal's success gave her "an opportunity to gratify my taste by meeting great numbers of them."

Few First Ladies were as spontaneously well-liked as Mrs. Coolidge. Her gray-green eyes seemed always crinkled in smiles, and the White House staff swiftly concluded she was "ninety per cent of the Administration." She waved gaily to throngs of people in parades while dour Cal sat quietly next to her. Romping daily on the White House lawn with her dogs and a pet raccoon, Grace was both natural and endearing. When her portrait was painted with her white collie at her side, Cal was disappointed that the artist made her wear a red dress and not the favorite white one he had selected. Although friends knew buying clothes for his pretty wife was frugal Coolidge's only extravagance, he quipped it was cheaper, he supposed, to buy a new red dress than to dye the dog.

As the roaring twenties thundered on Cal sought election in his own right. He won the Republican nomination in 1924, but campaign plans were abandoned when his sixteen-year-old son, Calvin, Jr., died suddenly of blood poisoning July 7. Coolidge said on the tragedy later, "I do not know why such a price was extracted for occupying the White House."

Though he had not campaigned, Coolidge won a decisive victory. Grace came out of mourning more gradually than he, but in 1927, driven from the White House by a warning that the roof was unsafe, began planning the mansion's renovation. She combed storerooms for authentic furnishings and antiques, persuading Congress to pass legislation so appropriate gifts could be accepted. Though few pieces were offered, she acquired some fine things for the Green Room and left her stamp on at least one other room. The "Sky Parlor" sun-room became a favorite retreat for her and later First Ladies. Grace's personal gift to the White House was a spread, which she crocheted herself for the Lincoln bed during her years as First Lady.

No one minded that Mrs. Coolidge deferred to her husband in almost every matter, for she took obvious joy in their relationship. She said, "I have scant patience with a man of whom his wife says, 'He never gave me a cross word in his life.'. . .If a man amounts to much in this world, he must encounter many and varied annoyances whose number mounts as his effectiveness increases." She loved teasing Cal, and her humor was often a match for his own. Knowing he disapproved of her giving press interviews, she accepted the invitation of newswomen to address them, then rose and gave a five-minute speech—in sign language.

The entire nation, including Grace Coolidge, was taken by surprise when Calvin announced, "I do not choose to run for President in 1928." Grace responded, "I am rather proud of the fact that after nearly a quarter of a century of marriage my husband feels free to make his decisions and act on them without consulting me or giving me advance information concerning them."

In 1933, four years after his retirement, Calvin Coolidge died. Grace, still responding to people and their needs, renewed her ties with the Clarke Institute, serving for two decades with other dedicated workers like Helen Keller and Christian Herter. When she died in 1957 at the age of seventy-eight, she asked that the Coolidge homestead in Plymouth Notch, scene of the "Lamplight Inaugural," be given to the State of Vermont. Her grave nearby marks a spot where Grace once found "peace which passeth understanding."

67

# 32
## Lou Hoover

### A New Breed

"I never entertain, I just ask people to come in and see us," Lou Hoover had said, and when she and Herbert moved into the White House March 4, 1929, nearly two thousand people joined them for lunch. It was a fitting beginning for an administration that had promised "two chickens in every pot," for the wealthy Hoovers, bolstered by the country's prosperity, provided "the best table that was ever set at the White House."

The new First Lady was pleased to be mistress of the Executive Mansion, which she had described as the most beautiful home in the world. She felt, however, that much could be done to improve it. Underwriting extensive redecoration, she initiated research for a complete history of White House furnishings. Continuing the search for antiques Grace Coolidge had begun, Lou herself unearthed the chairs pictured in a painting of Lincoln signing the Emancipation Proclamation. Her admiration for the Monroe furnishings was so great that she commissioned reproductions of select pieces for the Red Drawing Room upstairs.

Linguist, scholar, outdoorswoman and geologist, Lou Hoover seemed a new breed of First Lady, self-sufficient and astonishingly versatile. Herbert had realized what a rare girl she was shortly after they met in a geology class at Stanford University, when, on a field trip, Lou leaped a fence before he could decide how to help her over gracefully. Like Herbert, she accepted the tenet "there is that of God in every man," and her humanitarian instincts matched his own. While at Stanford Hoover courted the girl who shared his passion for geology and the outdoor life. After graduation he worked in gold mines in Nevada and Australia, waiting three years for Lou to finish her education before cabling, "Will you marry me?" She telegraphed "Yes," and Lou Henry became Mrs. Herbert Hoover on February 10, 1899.

Traveling became a way of life to the newly-weds. They honeymooned en route to China, where Hoover would be the emperor's mining consultant. In the provinces Lou followed Hoover's engineers on pack mule and canal boat. When the Boxer Rebellion threw Tientsin into chaos, she and Herbert took to their bicycles. Pedaling from one makeshift hospital ward to another. Lou nursed the wounded while Herbert organized defenses. Later, rescued by the Allies, Lou refused to leave until her patients had been evacuated.

The Hoovers were never idle, even in forsaken outposts or obscure villages. Utilizing every spare moment, they worked together translating from Latin to English the 16th-century folio, *De Re Metallica,* by Agricola. Even with Lou's superior linguistic abilities the task took several years.

Lou enjoyed globe-trotting and camping as much as her husband and was glad his work called for generous amounts of each. Even their two sons seemed to thrive on their trips. At one time, Hoover had homes as far apart as California, Washington, Mandalay and Tokyo.

They were in London, however, at the outbreak of World War I. Countless Americans found themselves stranded there, and at President Wilson's request, Hoover organized assistance committees. Later, Herbert undertook an even greater challenge—relief for the starving Belgians. Lou took her two sons back to the United States, then amplified Herbert's plea for the Belgians, crossing the country rallying supporters and funds. Joining her husband overseas, she helped establish the American Woman's Hospital. In 1919 in gratitude for her efforts King Albert conferred upon Lou the Cross of Chevalier, Order of Leopold.

As Hoover's reputation for organizational genius and humanitarianism grew so did his responsibilities. A self-made millionaire, he had worked during the war years without pay,

PAINTING BY RICHARD BROWN COPIED FROM PORTRAIT
BY PHILIP DE LÁSZLÓ, WHITE HOUSE COLLECTION

doing much to alleviate human suffering. Appointed Secretary of Commerce in 1921, he was one of the few officials untainted by the scandals of the Harding administration.

Lou loved Washington and enjoyed her role there though she disliked the custom of "at homes," a specific day each week on which wives of cabinet members were expected to receive callers. As First Lady she freed her own "cabinet wives" from such responsibility. Although she had no daughters, Lou Hoover was intensely interested in the Girl Scout movement. Later she served as president of the national organization, and during her years in the White House scouts were constant visitors.

Hoover's success as Secretary of Commerce under both Harding and Coolidge won him the Republican nomination in 1928 after Coolidge's "I do not choose to run" statement. An easy victor over derbied Democrat Al Smith, Hoover took office during the twenties'

last hurrah. The nationwide depression which followed the stock market crash did not drastically alter the Hoovers' preferred life-style in the White House, for they used their own money for lavish entertaining and a full complement of servants. Herbert, however, worked nearly around the clock in an effort to lift the economy and eliminate the shanty-town "Hoovervilles" springing up everywhere in a nation of unemployed. Realizing her husband needed a nearby place to relax that would not arouse public ire at a time of deprivation, Lou arranged for a summer camp for Herbert in the Blue Ridge Mountains. Camping at Rapidan on weekends, Hoover and his guests fished and built stone dams. Later, the Hoovers gave the complete camp, with its unique furniture which Lou had designed, to the Shenandoah National Park.

Despite all his efforts, the man who had fed millions of starving Europeans was unable to convince his own countrymen that prosperity was "just around the corner." Franklin D. Roosevelt's appeal for a "New Deal" carried the election of 1932 and the Hoovers left the White House under a dark cloud. Returning to Palo Alto, California, they lived part of the time in the dream house Lou had designed years before.

Though the country had turned its back on the "Great Engineer" and his wife, the Hoovers never abandoned the suffering and needy. During the Second World War they came to the aid of refugees, Lou working mostly through the Salvation Army. Queen Elizabeth of England appealed to Lou personally for clothing for London charities, and she responded with a successful national campaign.

On January 7, 1944, Lou Hoover died, leaving a letter for her husband and sons: "I am a lucky woman to have had my life's trail alongside the paths of three such men and boys." To Herbert, it was "the sweetest compliment ever given to men."

# 33
# Anna Eleanor Roosevelt

## First Lady of the World

"The turmoil in my heart and mind was rather great that night," said Anna Eleanor Roosevelt. Franklin had been elected President of the United States and "I knew what traditionally should lie before me." But Eleanor had eluded tradition in the past and did so again. Emerging as more than the President's wife, she became First Lady of the World.

Neither the presidency nor the White House awed the new First Lady. Her father's brother, Theodore Roosevelt, president at the time of her wedding, had given his favorite niece in marriage March 17, 1905. Eleanor loved and admired her uncle despite their political differences. Visits with him and Aunt Edith

PAINTING BY DOUGLAS CHANDOR, WHITE HOUSE COLLECTION

at Sagamore Hill had brightened an otherwise bleak childhood. Her mother had died when she was eight, her alcoholic father two years later, and Eleanor lived with her grandmother in a strict, somber household. Edith Roosevelt, drawn to T.R.'s awkward, self-conscious niece, wrote after one of Eleanor's rare visits, "Poor little thing. She is very plain. Her mouth and teeth seem to have no future. But the ugly duckling may turn out to be a swan."

In her late teens, a slim, striking 5 feet, 11 inches tall, Eleanor was neither swan nor ugly duckling. Several years abroad at the Allenswood School, under the sympathetic wing of a liberal headmistress, had quickened her mind and provided much-needed poise. An excellent student, she wanted to go on to college, but her grandmother insisted she make her debut instead. She had few beaux, but several young men seemed to enjoy her company and conversation. When one of them, her distant cousin Franklin Delano Roosevelt, handsome, eligible, and desirable, proposed, she was thunderstruck, gasping, "Yes!"

The new bride was taken in hand by Sara Roosevelt, Franklin's domineering mother. Malleable Eleanor belatedly recognized and tried to overcome Sara's enormous influence. She never fully succeeded, particularly where her five children were concerned. Sara spoiled them outrageously, even when they were grown, negating most of Eleanor's efforts to discipline her unruly brood. After five years of marriage Eleanor and Franklin temporarily escaped Sara's propinquity when they moved to Albany during his term as state senator.

Eleanor's social conscience awakened slowly as her husband's political career expanded. Exposure to people, all kinds of people, stirred her to action, and work for the fledgling Junior League broadened her horizons. The organization called for service, not just money for the poor, and Eleanor taught dancing at a settlement house. She also dragged Franklin through tenements, shocking him with housing conditions. As her focus shifted to the needs and wants of others, she overcame her feelings of inadequacy as a mother and daughter-in-law. The Roosevelt clan at Campobello and Hyde Park, their aristocratic friends and political cohorts seemed well able to take care of themselves. Eleanor began to champion those who could not.

But in 1920, when F.D.R. ran unsuccessfully for vice-president with James Cox on the Democratic ticket, Eleanor was still tottering on the brink of social commitment. Pushed into its mainstream by Franklin's attack of polio the following year, she brought the world to her disabled husband and found a new life for herself. "You're going into politics," Louis Howe, F.D.R.'s secretary told her, convinced that political bait alone would speed his chief's recovery. Eleanor brought Women's Trade Union League leaders to Franklin and she began speaking in public. Campaigning for Al Smith, she tempted Franklin with a reception for the gubernatorial candidate, and before long he began to seek further participation in the Democratic party again.

At the same time, Eleanor took up her own causes, dove-tailing them with Franklin's whenever possible. Convinced of the need for social and welfare legislation, she campaigned in 1926 for Senator Robert Wagner, who said she was the most important factor in his victory. With friends, she set up Val-Kill, an experimental, non-profit furniture factory near Hyde Park, giving jobs to the unemployed. She taught at the Todhunter School in New York and was named director for the Bureau of Women's Activities for Al Smith's campaign against Herbert Hoover in 1928.

Smith lost his bid for the presidency, but Franklin, running for governor of New York, was elected. When he ran for reelection in 1930 Eleanor worked behind the scenes at Roosevelt headquarters, feeling at that time it was undignified to campaign openly for her husband.

When Franklin went abroad to see his ailing mother in 1930, she wrote forlornly, "We really are very dependent on each other though we do see so little of each other. I feel as lost as I did when I went abroad. . . . Goodnight dear. . . . Dear love to you . . . I miss you and hate to feel you so far away."

Their marriage had apparently weathered the crisis of Franklin's involvement with another woman, Lucy Mercer. Few people outside the family knew of Roosevelt's relationship with Lucy, a well-bred, attractive young woman who had been part friend, part secretary to Eleanor. Stunned when she learned of the romance, Eleanor offered Franklin a divorce, which he refused. He did, however, promise to give Lucy up, and Eleanor was convinced that he had done so. Years later, she learned of his continued devotion to Lucy, who in time became Mrs. Winthrop Rutherford. Eleanor went on with the marriage nevertheless, commenting later:

All human beings have failings, all human beings have needs and temptations and stresses . . . . If at the end one can say: "This man used to the limit the powers that God granted him; he was worthy of love and respect and of the sacrifices of many people, made in order that he might achieve what he deemed to be his task," then that life has been lived well and there are no regrets.

In 1932, when the hard-won prize, the Democratic presidential nomination was Franklin's at last Eleanor sat nearby on the platform as he accepted the honor, saying, "I pledge you, I pledge myself, to a new deal for the American people." Planning to give up all her activities for the dignified role of First Lady, Eleanor envisioned a "new deal" for herself as well. Wistfully, she suggested she

71

might open the mail, unaware that during their years in the White House she would be the subject of most of it. "No, you can't help on the mail, Eleanor," Franklin replied. "But you will probably have some other things to keep you busy."

It took her just two days to find something. In the midst of the bank holiday, she announced regular press conferences for women reporters. Later, when the "Bonus Army" marched on the Capital as they had done during the previous administration, she went at Franklin's request to "talk to the boys." They soon dispersed, chanting "Hoover sent the Army. Roosevelt sent his wife."

Before long, Franklin was sending her everywhere as his "eyes and ears." He had his "Hundred Days" and she began logging hundreds of thousands of miles. As she hop-scotched the country reporting on labor conditions and minority groups, he called her his "Will O' the Wisp Wife." The Secret Service called her "Rover" and, unable to keep up with her, insisted she carry a gun.

Appalled by the poverty of a West Virginia mining town, she tried to set up a new community, but Arthurdale, her prefabricated project, was a fiasco. Construction inadequacies and mounting costs smothered the decency of her motives. Before the coal dust had settled on Arthurdale, Eleanor had become perhaps the most controversial woman in America. Likewise, her espousal of the American Youth Congress backfired when the organization was found to be communistic.

Among her successes, however, was the National Youth Administration, which she had fought so hard to help establish. Rescuing Ellen Wilson's faltering slum-clearance program, she put across the Alley Dwelling Act in 1934. She won equal pay for women from industries under the National Recovery Administration, and her long-time support for civil rights resulted in better employment op-portunities and desegregation of public facilities in the Capital. She gave more than lip-service to her belief in equality, inviting Negro contralto Marian Anderson to sing at the White House in February 1936. In 1939, when the Daughters of the American Revolution refused Miss Anderson the use of Constitution Hall because of her color, Eleanor resigned from the organization and arranged for the concert to be held on the steps of the Lincoln Memorial.

When F.D.R. scored his impressive second-term victory, Eleanor had become a strenuous campaigner. There was resentment, however, of her whirlwind fact-finding missions and her influence on the President. "My Day," a daily newspaper column she wrote, fanned the flames. At first criticized for being inane, it soon raised outcries of impropriety. Foreign powers grew as concerned about F.D.R.'s wife as they were about him. Mussolini called for an "embargo" on Eleanor, and in Germany propagandists said, "While President Roosevelt is trying to keep the United States out of war, his wife is trying to drag it in."

Meanwhile third-term talk had begun, and she told her husband, "You know I do not believe in it." Some suggested she run instead, pointing to an early 1939 Gallup Poll which showed that 67% of the public approved of Eleanor's conduct, while only 58% approved of Franklin's.

During the war, Eleanor kept careful watch on hiring practices in war industries. "I wanted to see the fight for the rights of minorities to go on during the War period," she said. When women began working in defense plants, she foresaw "an effect on the way of life and on the homes in the United States," recommending "day nurseries and play schools. . . transportation to both grade and high schools . . . community laundries."

When Pearl Harbor was attacked on December 7, 1941, defense on the home front

BROWN BROTHERS

The Roosevelt home at Hyde Park was dominated by Franklin's mother, Sara Delano Roosevelt.

seemed more than a remote possibility. Under New York's Mayor La Guardia, Eleanor accepted her first official government job: deputy director of the Office of Civilian Defense. But La Guardia's fears that she was "far too controversial" for the job were borne out. The OCD's inefficiencies and over-staffing were blamed on Eleanor, who resigned, saying, "I can't take a government position because of my being the President's wife. I found that out."

Distinguished guests from abroad joined the Roosevelts in the White House, among them King George and Queen Elizabeth of England, Winston Churchill, Madame Chiang Kai-shek, Queen Wilhelmina of the Netherlands, Charles de Gaulle, and foreign minister Molotov of the U.S.S.R. Eleanor, returning some of their visits, flew overseas, but stayed in more army camps than palaces, bolstering soldiers' morale. Swooping down on the South Pacific, she went to Guadalcanal against F.D.R.'s wishes and stayed in New Zealand, Australia and Nouméa.

She had opposed Franklin's third-term bid but did not argue with his fourth when he said, "I have as little right to withdraw as the soldier has to leave his post in the line." Interest centered on his choice for a running mate, with Eleanor preferring Supreme Court Associate Justice William O. Douglas. She had no objections, however, to Missourian Harry S. Truman when she read in the newspaper he had received the nomination.

Victorious over Thomas E. Dewey in November, F.D.R. left for Yalta soon after his Inauguration January 20, 1945. Home from the grueling conference, he rested at Warm Springs, the Georgia spa whose mineral waters had helped him regain much of his mobility. He died there suddenly April 12. Eleanor, informed of his death, was concerned for his successor and the nation. "The President has passed away," she told Harry Truman. "Tell us what we can do. Is there any way we can help you?"

A week later she had moved out of the White House, telling reporters who met her in New York, "The story is over." Franklin's perhaps, but not her own. Taking her up on her offer to help, President Truman appointed her a delegate to the United Nations in January 1946. There, as chairman of the Human Rights Commission, she was established as an independent thinker in her own right, beyond her husband's shadow. Asked to run for the Senate in 1946, she said, "I want to be able to say exactly what I please and feel free."

In 1948, she turned down those who wanted her to run for vice-president, saying, "I do not think we have yet reached a point where the electorate is ready for a woman vice-president who might possibly become president." She remained in the UN until 1952, where she was far more than what she claimed to be: "An old woman deeply interested in human problems and eager to help her country in any way she can." She remained a powerful force in the Democratic party, and was instrumental in Adlai Stevenson's successful bid for the presidential nomination in 1952 and 1956. She made a stirring last-minute appeal for Stevenson in 1960 as well, and challenged the bid of young John F. Kennedy.

When Eleanor died in November 1962 she was mourned by countless "little people" who had personally benefited from her charity and compassion. World leaders paid tribute to her abilities, though some had not always agreed with her methods or conclusions. Across the nation, millions wept, and even those who had disliked her agreed that a remarkable woman had passed away. Ahead of her time in social welfare and anti-discrimination legislation, Eleanor Roosevelt's imprint on American society is still keenly felt. She left, as Winston Churchill said, "golden footprints behind."

73

# 34
## Elizabeth Truman

### Independence Lady

Bess Truman hung up the telephone, her direct blue eyes blinded with tears. "President Roosevelt is dead," she told her daughter. Margaret later said, "Along with her grief for a great man and a good friend, she must have looked down the unknowable future and shuddered."

April 12, 1945, Harry S. Truman succeeded to the presidency, and his wife, the "independent lady from Independence," became First Lady. She was his childhood sweetheart, the girl he wooed for nearly thirty years before their marriage. "If I succeeded in carrying her books to school or back home for her I had a big day," chuckled Harry, who had discovered five-year-old Bess in Sunday school, "the prettiest, sweetest little girl I'd ever seen." Slim, fair-haired Bess Wallace loved baseball, always beat him at mumbly-peg and played a smashing game of tennis. Her family, well-to-do by Independence standards, lived in a spacious, many-gabled Victorian house called the Gates Mansion. Harry, the son of a farmer, was a persistent if unimpressive beau. Courting Bess, he commuted twenty miles on Saturday nights to see her, even before he had a car, later pressing his suit from Kansas City and a trench in France during World War I.

Though they were engaged before he went overseas, Harry delayed the wedding he had dreamed of for so long, explaining that he did not want Bess to find herself a widow or the wife of a cripple after the war. He returned in May 1919, and they were married barely a month later. Bess, thirty-four, and Harry, thirty-five, moved in with her mother at Gates Mansion. Two years later Harry's business, a Kansas City haberdashery, failed, and they were bankrupt. Harry was more successful in Jackson County politics, winning the support of the powerful Pendergast machine in a bid for the post of county judge. In 1926 he became presiding judge of the county court, later reinforcing his connection with Pendergast,

who helped him win election to the United States Senate in 1934.

The Trumans took a small furnished apartment in Washington, but Independence, Missouri, was always home. Bess liked Washington and quickly made friends there, but confronted with Senate wives' luncheons, said, "They bore me." She was glad to assist Harry again, having done behind-the-scenes staff work. Now, however, she was put on the payroll as his secretary at a $4,500 yearly salary. Harry told critics, "She earns every cent of it. I never make a speech without going over it with her, and I never make any decision unless she is in on it." When he headed a committee investigating waste in the defense program, compiling countless reports, he said, "Not one of these reports has been issued without going through her hands."

When Truman was mentioned as a possible running mate for F.D.R. in 1945, Bess was, Margaret Truman recalled, "bitterly opposed" to the idea. From a box on the sidelines, "looking tired and worried and as if she had been crying all night," Bess watched the Democratic National Convention nominate Harry. Surrounded by reporters, police, and Secret Service personnel, she turned to her husband and said, "Are we going to have to go through this all the rest of our lives?"

As First Lady, Bess felt the lack of privacy even more keenly. She immediately announced she would not continue Eleanor Roosevelt's policy of frequent press conferences. "I am not the one who is elected," she said firmly. "I have nothing to say to the public." When Eleanor Roosevelt left the Executive Mansion, one of its staff said, "This place needs a rest," and Bess Truman seemed to agree. She ran the White House as a home as well as the Executive Mansion, maintained protocol, and appeared publicly only when necessary. Harry said, "One of the biggest contributions she made was to see that the feminine part of the

BUREAU OF ENGRAVING AND PRINTING

View of the White House with the
Truman balcony added to the
south portico.

White House was run properly.... Certain
receptions were customary, certain programs
necessary. She did them all and was always
there to greet the guests."

Asked how she liked living in the White
House, Bess replied, "Oh, so-so," a comment
that seemed puzzling until it was reported
that one leg of Margaret's piano had sunk
tipsily through the floor, and odd structural
groanings went on in the venerable mansion
during the night. When a chandelier quivered
ominously during a reception, President Truman buttonholed the commissioner of public
buildings. His investigation revealed a danger-
ously deteriorating White House whose second
floor "was staying up there purely from habit."

With the East Room ceiling sagging a full
six inches, the Trumans were driven from the
White House. They moved across the street
to Blair House, where Bess set up a miniature
Red Room, Green Room and Blue Room.
While the White House was painstakingly
inspected and officials wavered between
saving the building or tearing it down completely, Bess expressed her own views to the
press in a rare departure from her customary
ladylike silence. The original walls, she felt,
should indeed be saved, and she was delighted
when the decision was made to retain them.

Bess said the most important qualities of a
First Lady were "good health and a well-
developed sense of humor." She saved her
tart witticisms for her family, however, feeling
public behavior should be more circumspect.
Her athletic ability was a constant source of
family humor, for she consistently beat
Margaret at tennis and ping-pong. When
Margaret teased her mother about having won
the shot-put at a track meet during her board-
ing-school days, Bess claimed the training
came in handy when she shook a thousand
hands a day. Her aim must have also been
good, for the White House staff nearly collapsed with laughter one night after dinner

when the Trumans snapped watermelon seeds
at one another.

Harry nicknamed Bess "Madame," or "The
Boss," asking her advice on all matters. He
said she was a "full partner in all my trans-
actions—politically and otherwise." Asked
if he had consulted her about the great decisions of his presidency, like the use of the
atomic bomb, sending troops to Korea, and
the firing of MacArthur, he replied, "I discussed all of them with her. Why not?"

Although she wanted to return to Independence as just plain Bess, she knew Harry
wanted to finish the job he had begun, and
so she whistle-stopped with him as he fought
the predicted Dewey landslide in 1948. Four
years later, Harry also welcomed retirement.
They returned to Independence to begin
work on his memoirs and the Truman Library.
President Truman, an enthusiastic student
of history, has said, "The proper role for
a First Lady is to be First Lady of the land.
That's what Mrs. Truman did. And she'll
always be First Lady as far as I'm concerned."

PAINTING BY GRETA KEMPTON, WHITE HOUSE COLLECTION

# 35
# Mary Eisenhower

## Ike's Mamie

As Dwight Eisenhower took the oath of office January 20, 1953, his wife Mamie burst into tears. Hearing her sobs, the new President crossed the Inaugural platform and kissed her in full view of the watching world. The enormity of Ike's responsibilities as president overcame her briefly, though during his campaign she had said, "What American woman wouldn't want her husband to be President?" But the General had been "on parade" for many years, while Mamie herself sported no rank. Suddenly she was First Lady and was heir to all its privileges and duties.

The privileges, she felt, outweighed the disadvantages. The presidency would provide her with the one thing she always wanted—a home of her own. Even if that home were the White House, she was happy to be in one place with at least a four-year lease. Her family had been on the move long before she became an army wife, for her father, a successful Iowa meat-packer, retired at thirty-six and moved his wife and four daughters west. They lived in Colorado Springs and then in Denver, wintering in San Antonio, Texas, where Mamie, whose real name was Mary, sporadically attended high school.

An afternoon jaunt to Fort Sam Houston, outside San Antonio, brought eighteen-year-old Mamie Doud under the steady gaze of Officer of the Day Lieutenant Eisenhower. Spotting a "vivacious and attractive girl," he talked her into joining him on his rounds. She was "saucy in her face and in her whole attitude," he grinned. As for Mamie, Ike was "the spiffiest-looking man I ever talked to. . . big, blond, and masterful." Popular Mamie, whom friends called a real "Rocky Mountain Belle," soon had time only for Ike. They were married less than nine months after they met, July 1, 1916.

The nineteen-year-old bride was delighted to be "looking after Ike," the only career she wanted. She kept house in "everything but an igloo," living in twenty-seven homes in thirty-eight years. She could decorate on a shoestring and move out of "shacks with cracks or palaces" at the drop of a salute. Her house-on-stilts in Panama boasted bats overhead and tarantulas underfoot, while at Marnes-la-Coquette, when Ike commanded SHAPE, Mamie ran a fourteen-room mansion and directed a bevy of French interior decorators. In Paris, "everyone" flocked to the Eisenhower's, and a nearby bridge over the Seine was dubbed "Pont Mamie."

"I knew almost from the day I married Ike that he would be a great soldier," she said, vowing to be unselfish and undemanding of her husband. "Being his wife meant I must leave him free from personal worries to conduct his career as he saw fit." She succeeded admirably, running the household, budgeting carefully, but always offering her hospitality to Ike's men and their wives. She provided just the right atmosphere to enable him to concentrate on his career priorities. In the Philippines she even tried to learn to play golf to encourage his relaxation with the sport.

But Mamie was not strong, and poor health curtailed her activities. She was hospitalized with a recurring lung infection when her two-and-a-half-year-old son, Doud Dwight, died of scarlet fever in 1921. "We were completely crushed," Ike said. "For Mamie, the loss was heartbreaking." In 1922 when she was expecting her second son, John, he wanted to transfer to the Army Air Force but did not, chiefly because of his concern for Mamie during her pregnancy.

For more than twenty years, Mamie had played the part of an army wife in a peacetime army. Then "war games" Ike had excelled in were no longer games, and travel, which had been so much a part of their lives, was suddenly restricted. December 7, 1941, Mamie recalled, "was the most terrible night of my life. Only when my little boy. . .died, did I suffer more." Pearl Harbor was only the first of many nights and days of anguish. Mamie was left behind in Washington during most of Ike's European "crusade," and her knowledge of events in the European theater was limited virtually to what she read in the newspapers. There was no question of risking interception of revealing letters. Ike wrote her nothing of his strategy. On D-day, news of the invasion did not reach Mamie until a reporter called excitedly to ask what she thought of the invasion. "What invasion?" Mamie had to ask.

When she joined Ike abroad after the war, she had to fulfill more than the routine responsibilities of an army wife. She was, in a sense, an American emissary. "From 1945 on," wrote the General, "Mrs. Ike and I had been moving in official circles all the time. In Europe there wasn't a royal family or head of government that she hadn't met and been entertained by." Mamie traveled to England, Holland, Belgium, Denmark and Sweden. She met the King of Norway, lunched with Queen Juliana at the Hague, and visited more than once with England's royal family.

Although both parties seemed ready to run Ike as their "conquering hero" candidate in 1948, Ike, for whom neither voting record nor party affiliation could be found, showed no interest in the presidency. Nor did Mamie, who commented, "When you're in the Army, you don't have politics." It was some time later that Ike declared himself a Republican. He accepted the presidency of Columbia University, a move that brought Mamie, whose higher education had consisted of a brief stint at a Denver finishing school, closer than she had ever been to a college. In 1950 he became supreme commander of NATO, and they left again for Paris. Even while in France, Eisenhower's desirability as a presidential candidate increased. Confronted with, among other

DWIGHT D. EISENHOWER LIBRARY

things, a substantial write-in ballot in a Minnesota primary, he decided to run. He returned home June 1, 1952, resigning from the Army to begin his campaign without "embarrassing the government or the Army."

Political tactics, he and Mamie soon discovered, could be as devastating as military ones. Taft supporters were intent on out-maneuvering the General, and the Republican convention was marred by contested delegations and procedural haggling. Mamie, watching the events on television, became visibly upset, so much so that she had to lie down in an adjoining room. She was still there when Ike's eyes, brimming with tears, told he had been nominated.

Under the circumstances, it was understandable that some of Ike's advisors feared Mamie's health might be a serious liability

77

in Ike's bid for the presidency. In addition to her bad heart, she suffered from Ménière's disease, a persistent inner-ear disturbance which caused frequent dizzy spells. But "Mrs. Ike" became nearly as great an asset to her husband as his famous grin. "I want you to meet my Mamie," he told crowds across the country, who stamped, shouted and whistled their approval of his little woman in bangs. Though she seldom said more than a dimpled "thank you" to the public, she generated grandmotherly warmth. Friends said because Mamie sincerely loved people, she instinctively put them at their ease, even in large groups. The grass-roots support for the couple was tremendous. By election day, even Mamie was confident. "I hope—no—I know—we'll win," she said before casting her own ballot.

Mamie thought the White House, its paint barely dry from the Truman renovation, "simply beautiful." She had "always looked upon it with a reverence and pride." Mamie was thrilled to have it become "a part of my life. . . .There is a wonder about living here," she said. Transmitting that wonder to others, despite her delicate health, was not easy. She rested sometimes until the last possible minute in order to stand for hours in a receiving line.

Mamie's excellent knowledge of food resulted in well-planned state dinners, and her love of flowers brought new floral beauty to the White House. She specified the day's menus and centerpieces herself and arranged for local hospitals to receive the flowers after her guests had left. She continued the sorting and identifying of the White House china collection, which for some time before the renovation, had been neglected. She felt personally responsible for the Executive Mansion, often making unannounced "white-glove" inspection tours. Despite her rigid standards, the staff thought her "very jolly" and called her "Mrs. Ike."

She took no part, however, in affairs of state and always excused herself when Ike discussed official business. When Ike did seek her advice, it was usually about people. "I frequently asked her impression of someone, and found her intuition good," he remarked. While Ike lay incapacitated after his heart attack in September 1966, Mamie made no attempt to serve as "regent" as Edith Wilson had during Woodrow's illness.

The President also suffered an attack of ileitis in June 1956, increasing doubt as to whether or not he would seek reelection. The First Lady when asked about a second term for her husband said, "The decision has to be made by only one person—Ike." He chose to run and Eisenhower's second election victory renewed their White House lease for another four years.

During his second term the President acknowledged the concern he also had for the health of Mamie. "We reduced our schedule after my heart attacks," he admitted, "because deep involvement in social activities made the day too long."

It was, of course, impossible for Mamie not to be affected by the crises that loomed during Ike's last administration, among them the U-2 affair, the U.S.S.R.'s successful launching of Sputnik, and the Hungarian revolt. It was not difficult to leave the White House for their Gettysburg farm, but the election of Democrat John F. Kennedy was a disappointment. Both Ike and Mamie were enormously gratified when, in 1968, Ike's former vice-president, Richard Nixon, was elected president, and grandson David married Nixon's daughter Julie.

When Ike died March 28, 1969, his last words were, "I've always loved my country." Years before, Mamie said she had tried to "match his spirit of personal sacrifice." Most people felt she had succeeded. In 1969 the Gallup Poll named her the most admired woman in the world.

# 36
## Jacqueline Kennedy

### Unbowed by Tragedy

Following her husband's election in November 1960, Jacqueline Kennedy said, "I feel as though I had just turned into a piece of public property." But in a sense she was already public property, for as a child of eleven she was praised in the *New York Times* for a "double victory in the horsemanship competition" at Madison Square Garden. She made headlines again in 1947 as "Deb of the Year," and a few years later was widely photographed as the fiancée of the Senate's most eligible bachelor, John F. Kennedy. She seemed to be just what her social secretary said she was, "A girl who has everything — including the President of the United States."

Jackie's was, however, no Cinderella story. The daughter of John Bouvier III, a wealthy stockbroker, and Long Island socialite Janet Lee, her pedigree was impeccable from birth. She summered at Easthampton, wintered in a Park Avenue apartment, and after her parents were divorced, enjoyed the Rhode Island estate and the Virginia hunt-country château of her stepfather, Hugh D. Auchincloss. Her education, too, was first-class; Miss Chapin's School in New York, Miss Porter's in Farmington, Connecticut, and Vassar. She fell in love with Europe when she summered there her freshman year of college, transferring to the University of Grenoble and then to the Sorbonne for her junior year.

Returning home, she continued her education at George Washington University, and after two more summers abroad, landed the "Inquiring Camera Girl" job on the Washington *Times-Herald* with the help of a family friend, *New York Times* columnist Arthur Krock. Assigned to interview Senator John F. Kennedy for her column, she rolled her eyes when her boss said, "Don't get your hopes up." She had met the senator before, at the home of a mutual friend who had been intent upon matchmaking. Although Kennedy later claimed he "leaned across the asparagus and

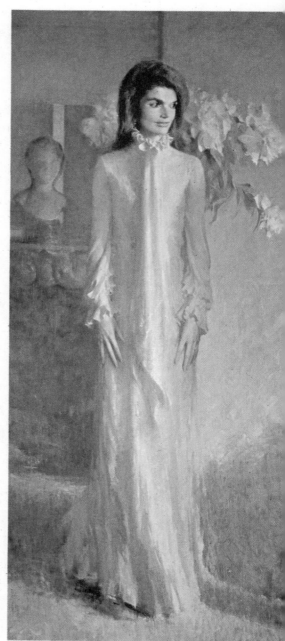

PAINTING BY AARON SHIKLER, WHITE HOUSE COLLECTION

79

asked the pretty girl for a date," Jackie countered that asparagus was not on the menu. But, she admitted, "It was more than just meeting someone. It started the wheels turning."

But the wheels turned slowly and privately. Jackie later broke a brief engagement to broker John Husted, Jr., a New York socialite, and announced she would marry Jack Kennedy.

Their wedding in September 1953 was a social extravaganza of twenty-six groomsmen and bridesmaids, 900 guests and several thousand gate-crashers, who nearly crushed the bride when they broke a police cordon.

As a senator's wife, Jackie showed no more interest in politics than she had previously. She had criticized Jack's "outlandish ambition" when they first met, for he made no secret of the fact that he wanted to be president, and she remained politically aloof even when his goal appeared within reach. Rumors that all was not well with their marriage died quickly when it became obvious that Jack enjoyed the chic, Continental change of pace Jackie gave him. He remarked, "I don't have to fight the day's political battles over again at night," and Jackie firmly declared, "Jack wouldn't — couldn't — have a wife who shared the spotlight with him." But Jackie herself seemed less certain of her role as First Lady, telling friends enigmatically before moving into the Executive Mansion, "Happiness is not where you think you find it."

At first her doubts seemed justified. Even during the campaign Jackie's designer wardrobe had drawn criticism. But the glamour of the most photogenic First Lady in memory carried the day. After the birth of John, Jr., in November she doffed her maternity clothes for a breathtaking collection of understated ball gowns, "Jackie pillbox hats," Chanel suits and easy-skirted dresses. At least one designer, Hollywood's Edith Head, called her impact on fashion "the greatest single influence in history."

Jackie's greatest disappointment in her new position seemed to be the White House. She told her husband, "It looks like a house where nothing has ever taken place." Long before the Inauguration she had done extensive reading and formed strong opinions about her new home. "The White House is an 18th and 19th century house," she said, and began immediate efforts to keep it as such. Jackie could not, however, undertake the renovation on her own, for by law, every change had to be approved by a commission. She created several committees of her own, appointing historians, art directors and museum curators to advise her. "Everything in the White House must have a reason for being there," she insisted.

While Grace Coolidge's similar plan for the restoration of the White House had met with little success, Jackie's was enthusiastically received. She sparked national interest in her project with an unprecedented television tour of the Executive Mansion and sponsored a bill to make the White House officially a museum, thus ensuring that gifts would remain there permanently.

Like many First Ladies, Jackie indulged her taste for ballet, theater and classical music. When Pablo Casals played for the Kennedys at the White House, as he had for Teddy and Edith Roosevelt, T. R.'s daughter, Alice Roosevelt Longworth, was invited.

An independent First Lady with ideas of her own as to what were "command" performances on her part, Jackie particularly admired Bess Truman's behavior as First Lady she said, because "she brought a daughter to the White House at a most difficult age and managed to keep her from being spoiled. . . . . Mrs. Truman kept her family close together in spite of White House demands, and that is the hardest thing to do." Jackie tried to do the same thing. She set up a play school

The Red Room after restoration and refurnishing of the White House interior begun in 1961 by Jacqueline Kennedy.

on the third floor of the White House so Caroline would have less public exposure and described herself as "livid" whenever her children's privacy was invaded by photographers.

Jackie did not welcome publicity for herself, either, but seemed to cause a sensation wherever she went, both at home and abroad. Awaiting the birth of her third child, she was glad to remove herself from the public eye, but when baby Patrick died she was more than ready to travel and campaign at her husband's side. Bronzed and rested from a recuperative cruise aboard the sumptuous yacht of Aristotle Onassis, she told Jack she would go with him on a political junket to Texas in November and promised that in the year ahead "We'll just campaign. I'll campaign with you anywhere you want."

Then, soon after the President's plane touched down in Dallas, Jackie's hot-pink perfection was shattered. Her blood-spattered figure inched over the back of the open car, hand outstretched to a scrambling Secret Service man after the assassin's bullets struck. She had cried, "They've killed Jack, they've killed my husband," then cradled his head in her lap as they sped to Parkland Memorial Hospital in a futile effort to save his life.

Barely an hour and a half after Jack Kennedy died, Jacquline stood pale but dry-eyed as Lyndon Johnson was sworn in as president aboard *Air Force One*. She had said, "Let them see what they've done to Jack," resisting all efforts to remove her blood-soaked suit and stockings and remaining composed while a shocked nation wept. During the next three days she sublimated her own tragedy in the interest of national dignity, walking gallantly behind her husband's flag-draped coffin, world leaders marching in her wake, and leading her children up the steps of the Capitol behind the bier. At Arlington National Cemetery she lighted an eternal flame at his grave, and when she left the

WHITE HOUSE HISTORICAL ASSOCIATION

White House in December, installed a memorial plaque in the presidential bedroom.

As the President's wife, Jackie had been idolized by millions. As his widow, her nobility staggered even those who envied her. But her marriage in 1968 to Aristotle Onassis, twenty-five years her senior, alienated many of her worshipers, who perhaps demanded eternal mourning for the widowed queen of the New Frontier. She became the jet set's "Jackie-O," surrounded by a retinue of personal servants and hairdressers. Widowed again after Onassis' death, that image persisted, fueled by published reports by former members of her staff who revealed intimate details of their mistress' life.

After Jack Kennedy's death Jackie had said, "So now he is a legend when he would have preferred to be a man." She, too, has become a legend, though there is no doubt she has always been first and foremost a woman.

81

# 37
## Claudia Johnson

### Lyndon's Lady Bird

The clock on board *Air Force One* in Dallas read 2:38 P.M. when Lyndon Johnson was sworn in as President of the United States. Seconds later his wife turned to Jacqueline Kennedy and murmured, "The whole nation mourns your husband." Lady Bird's face, taut with grief, reflected that national agony. "It has all been a terrible nightmare," she said. "Somehow we must find the strength to go on."

Lady Bird's own recuperative powers had been tested many times before, and no one who knew her doubted she would find that strength. She had lost four babies by miscarriage before daughters Lynda and Luci were born, but never indulged in self pity. When Lyndon served in World War II, she had kept his congressional office running in his absence, without pay, because she felt it was important to his constituents. Logging more time in Washington than any other presidential wife, Lady Bird had friends of every political persuasion and the respect and gratitude of countless charitable organizations for which she had worked. As the vice-president's wife she had been a popular goodwill ambassador. Now the tragedy of Dallas had thrust the Johnsons onto center stage and into new roles.

The new First Lady's "down-home" drawl and wide Texas smile brought warm reassurance to a grieving nation. The press and public found her nearly as hard to resist as Lyndon himself had, twenty-nine years earlier, when he proposed to the beguiling brunette after just one date. Although she turned him down, he was long on persuasion. Two months later, November 17, 1934, she married him, after her father commented, "Some of the best deals are made in a hurry."

The newlyweds lived in a tiny Washington apartment while Lyndon served as a congressional secretary. They moved to Austin, Texas, when President Roosevelt appointed Lyndon as Texas director for the National Youth Administration. They returned to Washington a year and a half later, after Lyndon had won a special congressional election to fill the vacancy left by the death of a Texas congressman. Lady Bird had financed his campaign, borrowing $10,000 against her inheritance, a legacy from her well-to-do mother, who died when Lady Bird was six.

In 1942 Lady Bird put more of her inheritance to work. A graduate of the University of Texas with a second degree in journalism, she had always wanted to own a newspaper, but decided a radio station would be a good substitute when debt-ridden KTBC in Austin was up for sale. She took over in 1943, investigating its weaknesses and strengths and going over balance sheets far into the night. She later acquired a VHF TV channel as well, and after twenty years, her original investment of $21,000 cash and a $10,000 bank note had grown to approximately $5 million.

Lady Bird's radio-TV venture and her wartime stewardship of Lyndon's congressional affairs were good preparation when she again stepped into the breach after Lyndon's 1955 heart attack. When he resumed his post as majority leader some six months later, his affairs were in good order.

Five years later, fully recovered, he made a try for the Democratic presidential nomination. When he lost the nomination to Jack Kennedy, Lady Bird said, "I'm relieved," but added "Lyndon would have made a noble President — a tough, can-do President."

Early next morning, Kennedy's surprise call with the offer of the vice-presidency changed their lives. Lady Bird said, "It was a very difficult decision. Lyndon's personality and temperament are not exactly suited to being a number two man." Nevertheless, Johnson decided to accept, and the strategy of his nomination boosted by Texas-size portions of Lady Bird's bluebonnet charm worked well for the Democrats.

When Jacqueline Kennedy's White House restoration and cultural projects emerged as "top priority," Lady Bird undertook the receptions and political trips that had previously fallen to the First Lady, as well as carrying out her obligations as Second Lady.

Later, as First Lady, she, too, had priorities, and by the time Lyndon had been elected president in his own right in 1964, she was ready to execute them. "I want to boast about America," Mrs. Johnson said, starting in her own backyard by creating The First Lady's Committee for a More Beautiful Capital.

Soon her environmental concern expanded to the entire nation. In the course of her "Beautification" program, she covered more than 200,000 miles, traveling by "rubber raft, bus, ski lift, surrey, orchard wagon, rail and foot."

The President's War on Poverty became her battle too, and she personally boosted the Head Start program for underprivileged preschoolers. She went to Newark, to Appalachia, to rural wasteland and urban ghettos. Her love for the sweeping Texas plains and skies did not diminish her concern for the future of American cities. She said, "The need for human understanding and kindness grows with the crush of our cities. We must expand not only our brains and our wits to meet the oncoming crises of metropolitan living, but enlarge our hearts to include all the occupants."

Women, she thinks, can do much to improve the world, though not by militant feminism. "The great effort of women is not, I believe," she says, "to invade a man's world or to create a woman's world but to be a full partner in a warm compassionate world." She perceives that "American women are undergoing a great revolution in our lifetime. We have learned to master dishwashers, typewriters and voting machines with reasonable aplomb. We must now try to make our laws

PAINTING BY ELIZABETH SHOUMATOFF, WHITE HOUSE COLLECTION

catch up with what has happened to us as we bounce in and out of the labor market and raise a family."

Johnson's decision not to run for reelection in 1968 had his wife's full knowledge and support. Reaction to the war in Vietnam and racial problems at home had forced his political withdrawal.

Home on their beloved Texas range at the sprawling LBJ ranch, the Johnsons worked together again, this time on the Lyndon Baines Johnson Library. Lady Bird's *White House Diary,* published in 1971, gave a remarkably detailed picture of her years in the White House.

The former First Lady had always considered her role as Lyndon's wife the cornerstone of her existence. "If I leave my footprints on the sands of time," she said, "it will be because he has been able to achieve something." But after his death in 1973, although she lived quietly at the ranch, her own humanitarianism and conservation programs received continued recognition.

# 38
## Thelma Nixon

### Hardworking Pat

OFFICIAL PHOTOGRAPH, THE WHITE HOUSE

Pat Nixon, reported the *New York Times,* looked "properly radiant" Inauguration Day, 1969. Richard Nixon had captured the presidency at last, and the bitter tears she had shed eight years before, when John Kennedy won the prize she thought was coming and had worked so hard for, were only a memory.

Hard work, however, had always been a way of life for Pat and Dick Nixon. Redoubling their efforts in 1968, their hard work paid off, as it had so many times before.

Nixon's background was humble, but his wife's even more so. The daughter of a Nevada copper miner, Pat saw near-poverty all around her. When the miner's disease, silicosis, struck her father, William Ryan moved his family to California and a small truck farm. There Pat, named Thelma but dubbed Pat in honor of her St. Patrick's eve birthday, helped in the fields, and when her mother died she took care of her father and two brothers. Four years later, when she was seventeen, her

father died. Left alone, Pat finished high school, worked in a bank and then, hoping to find better employment in the East, drove a family to New York. There she worked at Seton Hospital and in two years had saved enough as a secretary and x-ray technician to enter the University of Southern California.

She could not be a full-time student, however, and supported herself with available odd jobs. The most glamorous and lucrative was that of movie extra. She appeared in "Ben Hur," "Becky Sharp," "The Great Ziegfeld," and "Small Town Girl." When movie contracts were offered, she turned them down despite the tempting salary. "I wanted to finish my education. This meant more to me than quick money," she declared.

Education seemed to be the right answer for Pat Ryan. She graduated from the university with honors, then landed an excellent high school teaching position in Whittier. She coached cheerleaders, directed school plays, and gravitated to the town's little theater. There she met Dick Nixon, a young lawyer. He was playing in *Dark Tower*, a production Pat was to star in, and after the first rehearsal, he proposed to the pretty high school teacher. It was two years, however, and many long walks on the beach later before popular Pat Ryan agreed to marry him. "It was a fine wedding," said Pat, recalling the Quaker ceremony in Riverside June 21, 1940.

In 1941 the newlyweds left Whittier for Washington, where Dick worked for the Office of Price Administration. After he went on active naval duty in the South Pacific, Pat herself worked for the OPA in San Francisco until his return.

By 1946 the Nixons had both a daughter and a congressional seat. Pat had been neutral about Dick's running for Congress and recalled that during their courtship and early years of marriage, "there was no talk of political life at all." During leisure moments in

Washington, they bicycled beneath the cherry blossoms with Tricia, and later Julie. In Congress, Dick helped build a case against Alger Hiss. By 1950 Nixon was elected to the Senate with a reputation as a ruthless, hard-hitting campaigner. Pat had helped from the very beginning and virtually ran his office.

Pat's misgivings when Nixon accepted the vice-presidential nomination in 1952 seemed to be well-founded when the story of a "secret Nixon fund" for their living expenses made headlines, and many party leaders advised him to resign from the Eisenhower ticket. But Nixon bared his soul and his bank statements to the public. Eisenhower, watching his running mate's emotion-charged "Checkers" speech, decided to keep Nixon on the ticket.

John Kennedy's "eyelash" defeat of her husband four years later was a disappointment to Pat, but his election to the presidency at last in 1968 was clearly a moment of triumph. Reelection by a landslide in 1972 brought her supreme happiness. As First Lady, Pat Nixon was reluctant to embrace a project like Jackie's White House restoration or Lady Bird's "Beautification" program, although she quietly continued these activities of her predecessors. Without fanfare, she acquired some extremely important paintings for the White House, including two Gilbert Stuarts, one of Dolley Madison which had hung in the White House before its burning in 1814, and a portrait of Louisa Catherine Adams, John Quincy Adams' wife. Wanting to share the national treasures of the Executive Mansion with as many people as possible, Mrs. Nixon initiated White House tours for the blind. "They're allowed to touch," she said proudly.

The undisputed triumphs of the Nixon Administration on a national level, the "winding down" and eventual cessation of the Vietnam War and the reestablishment of diplomatic relations with the People's Republic of China brought great satisfaction to the First Lady. But her pleasure in those achievements was not only short-lived, but lost forever in the greatest presidential scandal of all time.

In 1972 when the first *Washington Post* reports of the Watergate break-in were published, Mrs. Nixon, as was her habit, followed the news avidly. Members of her staff recalled she never discussed Watergate, but seemed shocked and saddened with what she felt was an attempt once again to destroy her husband. H. R. Haldeman, she felt, was to blame, and she, who had never liked him, did not see him again.

A virtual prisoner of the White House, she carried on. She continued work with White House Curator Clement Conger on acquisitions and restorations. Outspoken in his regard for her, Conger recalls, "I have worked for six or seven First Ladies, and I admire Mrs. Nixon much more than all the others. She never let the altitude of the job go to her head. She was always just Pat Nixon from Whittier, California. She's so real, so warm, so realistic, so matter-of-fact. She did more for the authentic refurbishing of the White House, and its beautification, than any other Administration in history — and that includes the Kennedys. I only hope that someday she'll be given credit for her accomplishments."

To stand by while her husband announced his resignation and left the White House must have been an unbearable experience for Pat Nixon, whose steadfast loyalty and courage had been unfaltering. Many in the press and the public who had at one time been lukewarm to the woman referred to as "plastic Pat" changed their opinion. When she suffered a partial stroke in 1976 the public outpouring of sympathy and kindness was phenomenal.

President Nixon, it seems, described Pat correctly during his Administration when he called her "the woman of strength and character who stands behind the President."

# 39
## Betty Ford

### Devoted Teammate

In the East Room of the White House, just a few hours after Richard Nixon's emotional farewell, Gerald Ford took the oath of office as President of the United States. Afterward, he turned to his wife, Betty, kissed her on both cheeks, and proclaimed to the nation, "I am indebted to no man and only to one woman — my dear wife — as I begin this very difficult job."

Just how difficult neither would have guessed, though both were keenly aware that Jerry, the first vice president to succeed to the presidency not elected as part of a presidential ticket, was in a sensitive position. He had been Nixon's choice to succeed Spiro Agnew and was confirmed only after an exhaustive Senate investigation. However, the new President spoke confidently when he said in his Inaugural Address, "My fellow Americans, our long national nightmare is over."

But if the nightmare of Watergate was indeed ended at last, neither were the new President and First Lady living in a dream world. It had been, after all, less than a year since Gerald Ford had been named vice president, a post his wife never expected him to hold. She viewed the possibility of his succeeding to the presidency as remote and impeachment or resignation as a "terrible thing for the whole world." Terrible or not, it came to pass.

Most people might say Betty's life had already been extraordinary, for she had danced in Martha Graham's troupe, modeled for John Robert Powers and was the striking wife of Gerald Ford, successful Michigan congressman and House minority leader.

It was a far cry from her schooldays in Grand Rapids, when Betty Bloomer's friends, to her dismay, sometimes called her "Betty Pants." She showed an early determination to make something of herself, however, and an interest in the dance which began when she was eight opened many doors. At sixteen, she joined Martha Graham's classes at Ben-

OFFICIAL PHOTOGRAPH, THE WHITE HOUSE

nington College in Vermont for the summer, then returned the following year. She practiced hours daily, then taught others. Betty said of those days, "That was a fantastic time. We lived, breathed and ate dance . . . I was so excited I hardly slept."

The excitement lingered, for later she joined the Martha Graham troupe in New York. Betty found the great dancer a hard taskmaster. "I got many a knee in the back," she recalls, but insists the training was good for her. "More than anyone else, she shaped my life." Some years later she found that same drive to perfection in her husband.

Betty was well aware of the importance of work in a person's life, for her own had mattered deeply to her for many years. Martha Graham had urged Betty to make dancing her life, giving up everything else. "Stay, you've got the makings," she said. Betty thought it over for a long time but decided to return home where she launched a new career as a fashion coordinator. A marriage to William Warren, a furniture salesman, ended in divorce after four years on grounds of incompatibility. Betty received a settlement of $1 and an invaluable attitude toward her marriage to Gerald Ford. "I certainly learned, and probably appreciate more, what a good marriage can mean," she declared.

A few years later, she met Gerald Ford, the University of Michigan's handsome All-American and Yale Law School graduate who had returned to Grand Rapids. "The first time he asked me for a date, I refused him," Betty recalls. "I was working that night as a model at a fashion show, but he convinced me that I would be refreshed if I took a break."

By the spring of 1948, he had convinced her to marry him as well, planning an October 15 wedding in the midst of his first political campaign. Successful in his bid for a seat in Congress, Jerry took his bride to Washington. A veteran congressman's wife said of the representative from Michigan and his wife, "Now there's a couple that will go far."

Congress, however, seemed far enough, for Jerry's ambitions continued to center on the House of Representatives. Strenuous campaigning on behalf of fellow Republicans pointed towards hopes that his party's majority might lead to the post of Speaker. Betty's own career was now that of a busy wife and mother, caring for a growing family of three sons and a daughter and acting as a father some 200 days out of the year when Jerry was campaigning or on congressional trips. When Drew Pearson wrote that the Gerald Fords were in the Far East, Betty recalls that Jerry was there, "but I was right here, chauffeuring and cooking."

Suddenly, long periods of pain and partial paralysis set in, the result of a pinched nerve in her neck, an injury brought on by struggling with a stubborn window sash and aggravated by prolonged tension. Betty gave up dancing, underwent traction and a variety of physical therapy treatments with little relief. Finally, her doctor, convinced the strain she had been under caring for her family and coping with demands on Jerry was part of the problem, recommended a psychiatrist. "Just talking about the frustrations definitely helped," Betty says. "The psychiatrist suggested that I shouldn't give up everything for Jerry and the children, that I had also to think about the things that mattered to *me!*"

What mattered to Betty, however, paled beside the nation's agonies as the shadow of Watergate passed over the White House. Jerry's selection as vice-president and succession to the presidency put an end to his plan for retirement from politics, and the companionable home life the Fords had begun to savor was exchanged for the demanding role of First Family.

Just before moving into the White House Betty Ford had said, "This house has been like a grave. I want it to sing." Making it sing, however, would take more hope and prayers than she then realized. Stricken with breast cancer not long after moving into the Executive Mansion, the new First Lady underwent surgery, then candidly discussed her illness so that others might profit by her experience.

Despite her illness, Mrs. Ford succeeded in being the kind of First Lady she had hoped to be, a "public person," and one, moreover, widely praised and admired for personal courage. Forthright and candid, she spoke out for the Equal Rights Amendment. Jerry's failure to be elected president in his own right was a disappointment, but it was not without its consolations. She had said before his appointment that "for a few years I want Jerry to myself." That wish, at last, was fulfilled.

# 40
## Rosalynn Carter

### The Steel Magnolia

During the last week of the 1976 election campaign, Rosalynn Carter said, "When I come home this Monday night and unpack my suitcase, I'm going to put it in the attic for two months."

And just two months it was, for during the Inaugural ceremony January 20, 1977, the Carters' books, clothing and personal possessions were moved into the White House, completing the smooth transition between the Ford and Carter Administrations.

It was not the first time Rosalynn and Jimmy had left their home in Plains, Georgia, where their families had lived for two centuries. This time, however, all the world was watching. Neither the new First Lady nor her husband, however, seemed overly impressed with their new station in life. Humble beginnings, after all, had not deterred some of their predecessors in the White House.

"My father was a mechanic and my mother was a seamstress," Rosalynn recalled. "We were very, very poor, and we worked very hard." Just thirteen when her father died, Rosalynn Smith took care of herself and the three younger children after school while her mother worked in the post office and took in sewing. At fifteen, she went to work herself in a beauty parlor. Even while attending Georgia Southwestern College, Rosalynn lived at home and continued to help her family.

Living at home, of course, wasn't all drudgery. Pert and pretty, Rosalynn loved to dance and had many friends. One of them was Ruth Carter, whose older brother, Jimmy, was a midshipman at the U.S. Naval Academy. Rosalynn had had a crush on him since she was thirteen, and had never given up trying to make him notice her.

She finally succeeded when Jimmy, home on leave from Annapolis, asked her for a date during Christmas vacation. Later he told his mother, "That's the girl I want to marry!" They were married in Plains on July 7, 1946, just after Jimmy's graduation and commissioning as an ensign in the United States Navy.

Not yet nineteen, the new Mrs. Carter left Plains behind. She loved the travel of navy life and the opportunity to be on her own. "At that age, I hadn't seen the world, and I thought there was more to it than Plains, Georgia," she said. Her world expanded to include California, Hawaii, Virginia, Connecticut and New York, and three sons came along to fill those widening horizons as well. "When you're away from home and your husband's gone, you just have to take care of everything. And it was a good feeling for me. I liked it," Rosalynn recalled.

But the fun and travel stopped abruptly when Jimmy's father died in 1953. Jimmy and Rosalynn came back to Plains, where Jimmy took his father's place in the family peanut business. Rosalynn had misgivings about going back to Plains. She liked navy life, and she feared that a return to Plains would make her a little girl again. "I thought I'd come home and Jimmy's mother would tell me what to do, and my mother would tell me what to do."

But that didn't happen. Jimmy and Rosalynn took their own apartment, and Rosalynn went to work in the family business, doing the bookkeeping and figuring tax returns. She took a course in accounting, kept four sets of books and a master, and made everything balance. In peanut-harvest time she often worked from six in the morning until midnight. And she loved it, despite the hours, the strain and the fact that their first year's profit was just $187. Before long, Jimmy shared all business decisions with her. "I could advise him," Rosalynn explained, "because I kept all the books, I studied the tax laws, I knew everything that was going on and it was all exciting."

She did so well that when Jimmy decided to run for state senator and won, Rosalynn was able to take over the management of the business herself. His first, unsuccessful campaign for the governorship of Georgia, was their first joint effort that failed, and they plunged quickly into a long, four year campaign to win the second time around. Disappointed and depressed, Jimmy had turned to prayer, emerged refreshed and ready to make the second try. They were uplifted physically as well as spiritually by the birth of a fourth child, their first daughter, as Rosalynn reached forty.

"Amy made me young again," Jimmy said, and he and Rosalynn agree that the happiest night of their lives was not the night he won the presidency, but the night their daughter was born.

Winning the presidency however, was surely regarded as the greater accomplishment by the nation, if not the entire world, which was still saying "Jimmy Who?" on election eve, when Carter's early lead had shrunk to nothing, and most pollsters said the election was "too close to call." Rosalynn, once shy and reserved, had come to grips with her own retiring nature during her husband's successful campaign for governor in 1970. "People think we come from nowhere, but Jimmy *was* governor, you know," she said, and she had paid her own dues as a campaigner.

As First Lady, she quickly assumed much the same role she had played as Georgia's First Lady. "I learned when Jimmy was governor that I could do anything," she explained, from her "position of influence." Trusting her now, as he did then, Jimmy often sent her as his emissary. Soon, like Eleanor Roosevelt, the First Lady Rosalynn most admired, she became the President's eyes and ears.

He needed her more than ever when the American Embassy in Iran was besieged, and more than fifty Americans were held hostage. During the early days of the crisis, Carter confined himself to the White House and shunned campaigning. It was a position that soon came

OFFICIAL PHOTOGRAPH, THE WHITE HOUSE

to haunt him as time passed and the crisis remained unresolved.

Rosalynn, poised and confident, stumped again for Jimmy, speaking in her velvet-soft voice on women's rights, emphasizing her husband's record on this issue, stressing his commitment to human rights and racial equality.

In November they were dealt a stunning blow when the election that was "too close to call" turned into a defeat and several months later the Carter Administration passed into history. It was a hollowed-eyed Jimmy and a subdued Rosalynn who returned to Plains.

# 41
## Nancy Reagan

### Supporting Role

Inauguration Day, January 20, 1981, carried more with it than the traditional "old order changeth" certainty. This time, as one administration gave way to another, a delicate international situation hung in the balance and dangled there, midway between Carter and Reagan.

As the minutes ticked inexorably to twelve noon, Nancy Reagan, a tiny candle in flame-colored wool, a matching coronet in her hair, extended the well-worn family Bible and looked on adoringly as her husband, Ronald Reagan, former Governor of California and one-time movie actor, took the Oath of Office as the fortieth President of the United States.

As he stood facing West, Reagan seemed to emphasize his geographical and ideological roots. Yet the attention of the world turned East, not West, in those historic moments, waiting for Iran to release America's fifty-two hostages, still prisoners after 444 days of captivity. Twenty minutes later, they were free, and the President, too, was free of the terrible burden that had plagued the Carter Administration and sealed Jimmy Carter's defeat.

It was as if the sun had suddenly come from behind a great cloud, unleashing joy, patriotism and the return of the American dream. The new administration could be forgiven its white tie and tails, limousines and largess—it was clearly time to dance.

Indeed, despite inflation, high unemployment and serious economic concerns, the public seemed hungry for a return to glamour and style. The new First Lady seemed perfectly cast for the role the country had mandated for her.

It was Nancy who had brought the news that he was President, Reagan recalled. "My historic moment came," he said, "late in the afternoon in California when Nancy brought me out of the shower to tell me that the White House was calling. There I stood, dripping wet with a towel around me, listening to the President congratulate me."

Although she may not have dreamed her role would be so demanding so quickly, Nancy Reagan was well aware of the scope of her responsibilities. Citing Eleanor Roosevelt and Bess Truman, she acknowledged the differences in First Ladies. "One out front, one in back of her husband, both effective in their role," she said. "I guess I would be Nancy Reagan."

She was so well-suited for it, little media attention was paid to the fact that she was not the first, but the second wife of Ronald Reagan; his first wife had been actress Jane Wyman. He was the first President to have been divorced, an issue which may have cost other men the office. But Reagan said simply, "I think going on twenty-nine years of happy marriage to Nancy must settle it," and it did.

Nancy Reagan had given up her own acting career to marry her fellow actor and had obviously never regretted it. "I get annoyed during interviews when reporters, mostly women reporters, glare at me and say it's somewhat corny that I say my life began when I married Ronnie," she said. "I had had a career. I kept outside interests, but I wanted a family life. I still do . . . . Corny? If it is, great—but let's not keep knocking it, or pretty soon we won't have much left to respect in life."

Her role as First Lady would clearly be a supporting one, featuring the same devotion to her husband that had always characterized their life together. This loyalty to hearth and home was no surprise to those who knew her.

She was born Nancy Robbins, the daughter of a New Jersey car salesman and actress Edith "DeeDee" Luckett. When DeeDee's husband deserted her shortly after Nancy's birth, DeeDee went to work, leaving her infant daughter with sister and brother-in-law Virginia and Audley Galbraith in Bethesda, Maryland.

Aunt Virginia was kindness in itself, Nancy

admits, but as a child "you want your mother." It was true that Nancy went to stay with her mother whenever DeeDee had a role that kept her in New York for any length of time. "But I missed her," she said. As for her father, she was never close to him.

Fortunately there were other, happier memories. When Nancy was almost seven, DeeDee married a prominent Chicago neurosurgeon, Loyal Davis. To the little girl, he was "a man of more strength and integrity than any man I have ever known other than Ronnie." Loyal Davis adopted Nancy, who took his name and who always refers to him as her father.

Bitten by the acting bug like her mother, Nancy majored in drama at Smith College and headed for New York after graduation. Concerned friends of DeeDee's such as comedienne Zasu Pitts and actors Walter Huston and Spencer Tracy, willingly launched Nancy's career. Promising appearances in New York led to an M-G-M contract, and before long, pretty Nancy Davis left Manhattan for Hollywood and the lure of stardom. She ultimately made eleven movies, one of them "Hellcats of the Navy," with her future husband.

Director Mervyn LeRoy, who introduced them, may have had an ulterior motive, for he told Reagan, then divorced for four years from Jane Wyman, that Nancy was beautiful and he "might get to like her." Indeed he did. They were married shortly afterward, in 1952. The storybook romance and marriage soon included a son and daughter, a family which became Nancy's entire world.

This world came close to being shattered on March 30, 1981, a day on which Nancy was uncharacteristically absent from her husband's side. Ronald Reagan was the target of a would-be assassin whose bullet pierced the President's chest. It seemed as if the "curse of the zero" had struck again—the quirk of history that has felled every President elected in a year ending with zero since 1840.

OFFICIAL PHOTOGRAPH, THE WHITE HOUSE

In some ways, his recovery seemed faster than her own. Feeling guilty at not having been with him that day and clearly willing to have suffered for him, she went through a difficult time.

There was no question of her "taking over the reins" as did Mrs. Woodrow Wilson; no public display of any kind. She remained the fiercely private person she had always said she was, putting husband and children first.

Ronald Reagan has no doubt as to just who Nancy Reagan is, for she has been dedicated to him for nearly three decades. "She is very much what you see," he says. "I miss her very much when we're not together. We're very happy. I imagine if I sold shoes, as my father did, she would have wanted to help me sell shoes."

* OUR NEWEST FIRST LADY — Nancy Davis Reagan was born in New York City in 1921. She married Ronald Reagan in 1952 and had two children, a daughter and a son. A previous marriage by Ronald Reagan to actress Jane Wyman ended in divorce in 1948. The couple had a daughter and adopted a son.

# Comparative Data on Wives of the Presidents

| Wives of the Presidents | Birthplace | Born | Married | Died | Age | Sons | Daughters |
|---|---|---|---|---|---|---|---|
| 1. Martha Dandridge [Custis] Washington[1] | New Kent Co., Va. | 1731 | 1759 | 1802 | 70 | two[2] | two[2] |
| 2. Abigail Smith Adams | Weymouth, Mass. | 1744 | 1764 | 1818 | 73 | three | two |
| 3. Martha Wayles [Skelton] Jefferson[3] | Charles City Co., Va. | 1748 | 1772 | 1782 | 33 | two[4] | five |
| 4. Dolley Payne [Todd] Madison[5] | Guilford Co., N. C. | 1768 | 1794 | 1849 | 81 | two[2] | .... |
| 5. Elizabeth Kortright Monroe | New York, N. Y. | 1768 | 1786 | 1830 | 62 | one | two |
| 6. Louisa Catherine Johnson Adams | London, England | 1775 | 1797 | 1852 | 77 | three | one |
| 7. Rachel Donelson [Robards] Jackson[6] | Halifax Co., Va. | 1767 | 1791 | 1828 | 61 | .... | .... |
| 8. Hannah Hoes Van Buren | Kinderhook, N. Y. | 1783 | 1807 | 1819 | 35 | four | .... |
| 9. Anna Symmes Harrison | Morristown, N. J. | 1775 | 1795 | 1864 | 88 | six | four |
| 10. Letitia Christian Tyler | New Kent Co., Va. | 1790 | 1813 | 1842 | 51 | three | five |
| 11. Julia Gardiner Tyler | Gardiner's Isl., N. Y. | 1820 | 1844 | 1889 | 69 | five | two |
| 12. Sarah Childress Polk | Murfreesboro, Tenn. | 1803 | 1824 | 1891 | 87 | .... | .... |
| 13. Margaret Smith Taylor | Calvert Co., Md. | 1788 | 1810 | 1852 | 63 | one | five |
| 14. Abigail Powers Fillmore | Stillwater, N. Y. | 1798 | 1826 | 1853 | 55 | one | one |
| 15. Caroline Carmichael [McIntosh] Fillmore[7] | Morristown, N. J. | 1813 | 1858 | 1881 | 67 | .... | .... |
| 16. Jane Appleton Pierce | Hampton, N. H. | 1806 | 1834 | 1863 | 57 | three | .... |
| 17. Mary Todd Lincoln | Lexington, Ky. | 1818 | 1842 | 1882 | 63 | four | .... |
| 18. Eliza McCardle Johnson | Leesburg, Tenn. | 1810 | 1827 | 1876 | 65 | three | two |
| 19. Julia Dent Grant | St. Louis, Mo. | 1826 | 1848 | 1902 | 76 | three | one |
| 20. Lucy Webb Hayes | Chillicothe, Ohio | 1831 | 1852 | 1889 | 57 | seven | one |
| 21. Lucretia Rudolph Garfield | Hiram, Ohio | 1832 | 1858 | 1918 | 85 | five | two |
| 22. Ellen Herndon Arthur | Fredericksburg, Va. | 1837 | 1859 | 1880 | 42 | two | one |
| 23. Frances Folsom Cleveland[8] | Buffalo, N. Y. | 1864 | 1886 | 1947 | 83 | two | three |
| 24. Caroline Scott Harrison | Oxford, Ohio | 1832 | 1853 | 1892 | 60 | one | one |
| 25. Mary Lord [Dimmick] Harrison[9] | Honesdale, Pa. | 1858 | 1896 | 1948 | 89 | .... | one |
| 26. Ida Saxton McKinley | Canton, Ohio | 1847 | 1871 | 1907 | 59 | .... | two |
| 27. Alice Lee Roosevelt | Chestnut Hill, Mass. | 1861 | 1880 | 1884 | 22 | .... | one |
| 28. Edith Carow Roosevelt | Norwich, Conn. | 1861 | 1886 | 1948 | 87 | four | one |
| 29. Helen Herron Taft | Cincinnati, Ohio | 1861 | 1886 | 1943 | 82 | two | one |
| 30. Ellen Axson Wilson | Savannah, Ga. | 1860 | 1885 | 1914 | 54 | .... | three |
| 31. Edith Bolling [Galt] Wilson[10] | Wytheville, Va. | 1872 | 1915 | 1961 | 89 | .... | .... |

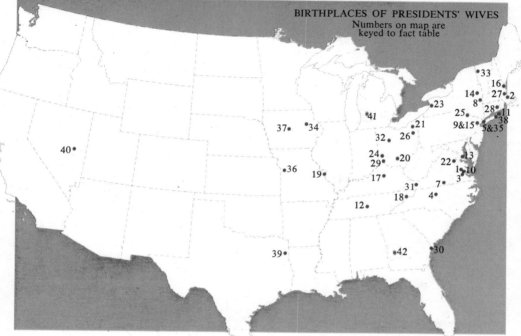

BIRTHPLACES OF PRESIDENTS' WIVES
Numbers on map are
keyed to fact table

| Wives of the Presidents | Birthplace | Born | Married | Died | Age | Sons | Daughters |
|---|---|---|---|---|---|---|---|
| 32. Florence Kling [De Wolfe] Harding[11] | Marion, Ohio | 1860 | 1891 | 1924 | 64 | one[2] | .... |
| 33. Grace Goodhue Coolidge | Burlington, Vt. | 1879 | 1905 | 1957 | 78 | two | .... |
| 34. Lou Henry Hoover | Waterloo, Iowa | 1875 | 1899 | 1944 | 68 | two | .... |
| 35. Anna Eleanor Roosevelt | New York, N. Y. | 1884 | 1905 | 1962 | 78 | five | one |
| 36. Elizabeth Wallace Truman | Independence, Mo. | 1885 | 1919 | ........ | .... | .... | one |
| 37. Mary (Mamie) Doud Eisenhower | Boone, Iowa | 1896 | 1916 | ........ | .... | two | .... |
| 38. Jacqueline Bouvier Kennedy[12] | Southampton, N. Y. | 1929 | 1953 | ........ | .... | two | one |
| 39. Claudia (Lady Bird) Taylor Johnson | Karnack, Tex. | 1912 | 1934 | ........ | .... | .... | two |
| 40. Thelma (Patricia) Ryan Nixon | Ely, Nev. | 1912 | 1940 | ........ | .... | .... | two |
| 41. Elizabeth Bloomer (Warren) Ford[13] | Grand Rapids, Mich. | 1918 | 1948 | ........ | .... | three | one |
| 42. Rosalynn Smith Carter | Plains, Ga. | 1927 | 1946 | ........ | .... | three | one |

[1] Widow of Col. Daniel Parke Custis
[2] Children from first marriage
[3] Widow of Bathurst Skelton
[4] One son from first marriage
[5] Widow of John Todd, Sr.

[6] Divorcee of Capt. Lewis Robards
[7] Widow of Ezekiel C. McIntosh
[8] Remarried in 1913 to Thomas J. Preston, Jr.
[9] Widow of Walter Erskine Dimmick

[10] Widow of Norman Galt
[11] Divorcee of Henry De Wolfe
[12] Remarried in 1968 to Aristotle Onassis
[13] Divorcee of William Warren

91

# Index